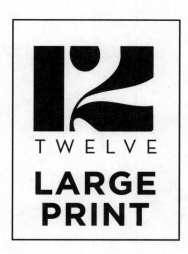

TWELVE

LARGE
PRINT

A
WARNING

Anonymous

A Senior Trump Administration Official

TWELVE

LARGE PRINT

Twelve
Hachette Book Group
1290 Avenue of the Americas
New York, NY 10104
twelvebooks.comtwitter.com/twelvebooks

First Edition: November 2019

Twelve is an imprint of Grand Central Publishing. The Twelve name and logo are trademarks of Hachette Book Group, Inc.

The publisher is not responsible for websites (or their content) that are not owned by the publisher.

The Hachette Speakers Bureau provides a wide range of authors for speaking events. To find out more, go to www.hachettespeakersbureau.com or call (866) 376-6591.

Library of Congress Cataloging-in-Publication Data
has been applied for.

ISBNs: 978-1-5387-1846-9 (hardcover), 978-1-5387-1847-6 (ebook)
978-1-5387-3546-6 (large print)

Printed in the United States of America

LSC-C

10 9 8 7 6 5 4 3 2 1

To my children, and the forthcoming generation, whose responsibility it will be to ensure freedom's torch remains lit and—as many Americans have before them—undertake that it be passed to the next.

Contents

"Character, in the long run, is the decisive factor in the life of an individual and of nations alike."

—Theodore Roosevelt

A WARNING

INTRODUCTION

*"Here in America we are descended in blood
and in spirit from revolutionaries and rebels—
men and women who dared to dissent from
accepted doctrine. As their heirs, may we never
confuse honest dissent with disloyal subversion."*
—*Dwight D. Eisenhower*

The Donald J. Trump administration will be remembered as among the most tumultuous in American history. Future historians will record the volatility of the president's decision-making, as well as the internal struggles of a government forced to grapple with it. They will write that his advisors came to find him unfit for the job. He couldn't focus on governing, and he was prone to abuses of power, from ill-conceived schemes to punish his political rivals to a propensity for undermining vital American institutions. They will document how officials considered drastic—some might say desperate—measures to warn the American people. During the Watergate scandal, key government leaders

1

quit in protest of President Richard Nixon's inappropriate activities. The press dubbed it the "Saturday Night Massacre." What is not known is that the same measure was considered less than halfway into the Trump administration, as top advisors and cabinet-level officials contemplated what might be called a midnight self-massacre, resigning en masse to call attention to Trump's misconduct and erratic leadership. The idea was abandoned out of fear that it would make a bad situation worse. It got worse anyway. Full awareness of the deteriorating state of affairs dawned on me late one evening, when the loss of a good man revealed the true nature of a troubled one. It was the evening that ultimately led to the writing of this book.

On August 25, 2018, John McCain, one of America's last great statesmen, died at home in Arizona. In the days that followed, the country mourned the passing of an American hero. McCain, a former military officer, first came to be known to the public for the five years he spent as a prisoner of war in Vietnam, where he was regularly beaten and tortured by enemy forces. One of his captors shattered his right shoulder. They broke his left arm. They cracked his ribs. In his agony, John contemplated suicide. For the rest of his life, he was unable to raise his arms to their full height due to his injuries and the after-effects of the torture. Yet when his captors offered him an early release, he refused until all other Americans captured before him were set free.

McCain finally was released in 1973. He was welcomed home by President Richard Nixon and later embraced as a Republican leader of the future by Ronald Reagan. He went on to build a vast legacy of public service as a member of the US House of Representatives, a senator, and a two-time candidate for president. At his funeral in Washington, DC, John was celebrated and mourned by a bipartisan crowd of government leaders, foreign heads of state, and millions of Americans who watched and listened nationwide.

"In one epic life," former president George W. Bush told the mourners, "was written the courage and greatness of our country." Former president Barack Obama took to the podium to herald McCain as "a patriot who embodied so much that is best in America." He added: "When John spoke of virtues like service and duty, it didn't ring hollow. They weren't just words to him. It was a truth that he had lived and for which he was prepared to die." A central theme echoed throughout the service. John McCain was a man of character, thoroughly committed to his principles and worthy of reverence, including by people who didn't always agree with him, or who he occasionally irritated with his stubbornness and persistence.

But one man did not share these sentiments. Instead of feeling somberness, he felt spite. Instead of respect, he offered resentment. That man was the sitting president of the United States. It was no secret that Donald J. Trump hated John McCain. "He is not a war hero," Trump remarked in 2015 to a stunned audience in Iowa. "I like people who weren't captured." Though he received McCain's support during the general election, then-candidate Trump bristled when the senator withdrew his endorsement in the wake of the *Access Hollywood* scandal, in which the businessman bragged about grabbing women's private parts, and he could not abide McCain's criticisms once in office.

It was no surprise that the president was agitated by the outpouring of public appreciation toward the senator. He is flustered whenever the spotlight shifts away from him, but especially if it moves toward a perceived rival, even a deceased one. What *was* surprising was the lengths to which he would go to settle the score. President Trump, in unprecedented fashion, was determined to use his office to limit the nation's recognition of John McCain's legacy.

After being lowered briefly on the day of the senator's death, the American flag atop the White House was raised the next evening. Aides worried this would send a bad signal, and tried to have it re-lowered. White House senior advisors implored President Trump to issue a proclamation for flags at all federal office buildings to remain at half-staff. They urged him to issue a formal statement on the late senator's death and legacy. These few gestures are standard protocol by any president when a distinguished senator dies, regardless of their party, as a sign of respect for the office and a demonstration that some things come ahead of partisanship. President Trump rebuffed each request. In fact, he wanted all government buildings to hoist their flags *back up*. Members of the staff were dumbfounded. Many among us had disagreements with John over the years, but we all honored his service to the nation as we would any person who wore the flag of the United States into battle and suffered at the hands of an enemy, let alone his later contributions to our country.

The standoff was broken not by a change of heart, but by public pressure. President Trump faced withering criticism for withholding support for McCain. Internally the temperature was rising. After frantic pleas from the communications team and increasingly bad television coverage, the president finally relented and allowed for a short statement to be drafted and for a proclamation to be issued. He also allowed administration surrogates to attend memorial services in his place. The flags, which by then most agencies had put at half-staff anyway instead of waiting longer for a presidential order, were finally lowered everywhere.

Less than two years into the Trump administration, this episode was almost unremarkable. By then Americans had grown accustomed to the president's pettiness, and they were numb to the endless controversies. Most probably tried to look the other way.

But I couldn't.

I'd spent enough time watching one pointless indignity after another. This one, targeting a veteran and former POW, was the last straw. What did it say about our president? What did it tell us about his values, virtues, and motives? Someone in the administration needed to say something, anything. There was silence. So the next morning I started drafting an op-ed about Donald Trump's lack of a moral compass and about the efforts of a group of administration officials trying to keep the government afloat amid the madness.

"I would know," I wrote of those officials. "I am one of them."

"Resistance" Revisited

Since that opinion piece was published in the *New York Times* on September 5, 2018, the instability within the Trump administration has intensified. One element has remained constant, however. The president still lacks the guiding principles needed to govern our nation and fails to display the rudimentary qualities of leadership we should expect of any commander in chief.

In the *Times* op-ed, I wrote of a quiet "resistance" of Trump appointees—at the highest levels—trying to manage his rash impulses. We wanted the administration to succeed and supported significant components of the president's agenda, but we were alarmed by his unstable behavior, in public and private. Those who tried to steer him away from self-destructive impulses were not the so-called "Deep State," I wrote, but the "Steady State."

This idea was assailed by the president. But the notion, that his team is working to protect him from himself, has since become one of the defining narratives of the Trump administration. Indeed, it was a hallmark takeaway from Special Counsel Robert Mueller's *Report on the Investigation into Russian Interference in the 2016 Presidential Election.* "The President's efforts to influence the investigation were mostly unsuccessful," he wrote, "but that is largely because the persons who surrounded the President declined to carry out orders or accede to his requests." This included the president's demand that White House counsel Don McGahn fire the special counsel, a request McGahn rebuffed for fear it would "trigger what he regarded as a potential Saturday Night Massacre" and lead to Donald Trump's impeachment. It probably would have.

President Trump should not be shocked that wary aides and cabinet members saved his presidency. My colleagues have done so many times. He should be worried—we all should be worried—that these reasonable professionals are vanishing. The president is chafed by those who dare to challenge him. He has targeted and removed many of these officials, from Secretary of State Rex Tillerson to Chief of Staff John Kelly, one by one. Others have grown tired of the charade and left of their own accord. With every dismissal or departure of a level-headed senior leader, the risks to the country grow, and the president is validated by a shrinking cadre of advisors who abet or encourage his bad behavior. We are already seeing the consequences.

The stewards of what I call the Steady State, what is left of it anyway, are public servants who push back against ill-considered or reckless decisions. They are not traitors or mutineers. They give the president their best advice and speak truth to power. They do not hesitate to challenge Trump when they believe he is wrong. They try to manage their White House offices or government agencies in a way that keeps them running despite the president's temperamental manner. When they fail to persuade him to change course, they work with the president and others in the administration to limit the fallout from decisions that will have deleterious consequences, which happens to be an enduring dilemma here inside the Trump administration.

Increasingly, I've doubted whether this type of environment is at all effective, let alone sustainable. Can Americans put their faith in a cabal of unelected officials to maintain stability? More importantly, *should* they? This question is more urgent than ever because there is a chance Donald Trump, despite his extraordinary flaws and the threat of impeachment in Congress, will be reelected in 2020. By then the guardrails will be gone entirely, and freed from the threat of defeat, this president will feel emboldened to double down on his worst impulses. This may be our last chance to act to hold the man accountable. Before doing so, we must look deeper at the roots of the present disorder, which is why I have written this book.

What This Book Is

The criticism of the Trump administration is so frenzied that ordinary Americans are struggling to discern truth from fiction. There is only so much the public can absorb. When everything is a crisis and a scandal, the end result is that nothing is. Americans are fed up with the cacophony, becoming numb to it. We are looking the other way, which has caused us to lose sight of what is important in the national debate.

I want to cut through the noise. I agreed to serve in the administration with the hope that President Trump would be successful and remembered for the right reasons, even if many of us had serious misgivings about signing on. While the president can claim a number of real accomplishments, overall that hope was dashed—and our misgivings validated—by hard experience. Through a toxic combination of amorality and indifference, the president has failed to rise to the occasion in fulfilling his duties. In these pages, I will underscore what Americans should actually be concerned about when it comes to Trump and his administration, diagnose the problems, and propose how we can move forward. The opinions presented herein are my own; yet, there is scarcely a criticism leveled that is not also shared by many other officials on the team or those who have departed. Most are afraid to say so publicly.

This book was conceived of, outlined, and written quickly amidst a flurry of fast-moving events and turmoil that is the norm in Trump's Washington. Nonetheless, it is focused on aspects of the presidency and this moment in our political life that are unlikely to change anytime soon. Each chapter highlights an aspect of the Trump presidency that I believe is essential for the public to consider as they decide whether to keep Donald Trump in office beyond 2020.

A great deal has been written to document the administration's chaos, an overused but unfortunately apt word. Some books have captured the atmosphere more accurately than others. Most of them have been authored by journalists and outside commentators who've only witnessed it secondhand or spoken to select sources, leaving readers to wonder how much of it is real and how much of it is "spin" promoted by people with an ax to grind. In these pages, I've done my best to provide an unvarnished assessment of Donald Trump and his presidency based on my own observations and experience, not baseless rumors. Certain content in this book will confirm existing reporting or put it in a more accurate light, some of it will be new, and many recollections will have to remain in my memory until the right time, lest the debate devolve into one about my identity, which I will discuss in a moment.

This text is written for a broad audience, not just for those already opposed to the president. Undoubtedly, his critics who read this book will feel justifiable outrage over its contents and greater unease about our nation's present trajectory. They will fear the costs of a reelected Donald Trump, and they are right to be concerned. Unsavory figures in his orbit have relished the possibility of another four years—not in the "we can do good for the country" way you would hope, but rather with the attitude that "no one will be able to stop us." I share your worry.

This text is also written with the hope that it might be given to the Trump supporter, or at least a subset of them. Many reasonable people voted for Trump because they love their country, wanted to shake up the establishment, and felt that the alternative was worse. I know you because I've felt the same way. I've worked with you. Many of you are my friends. But I also know deep inside you feel that something is not right about this presidency. That Donald Trump's behavior is not tolerable, and is often embarrassing. We have ignored what we didn't want to see. We've made excuses: "He's just got a different style." "He may be brash, but he gets it done." "The other side is worse." "The media is stacked against him." I shared those sentiments, but this book is in part an effort to demonstrate why excuses have blinded us to some ugly but necessary truths. I challenge you to withhold your reservations and read this to the end.

On Anonymity

Let me paint a picture of America. An exceptional country, founded with a clear sense of purpose, is conflicted and at a crossroads. Citizens are more divided than ever, right down to the household level, and sensational media coverage only compounds it. The rhetoric of politicians has grown coarse. Congress is dysfunctional. Public officials are at odds over how to fix the mess unlike ever before.

This may be the America familiar to you in the present day, but it is not the one I am describing. This was our country in the year 1787, when a roaring debate was taking place across the United States. Our young republic was beset with a weak central government that put national cohesion in danger. America's future was in doubt. All thirteen states sent representatives to Philadelphia for an emergency convention to discuss improving the Articles of Confederation to better unify the country. Instead of simply revising the Articles, secret meetings were held at the convention, leading to the creation of an entirely new governing document altogether.

Not everyone supported it. But with the backing

of thirty-nine of fifty-five delegates, a draft Constitution was released to the public for consideration and ratification. Approval was hardly certain. Two camps emerged: *federalists*, who wanted a stronger central government, and *antifederalists*, who preferred more power in the hands of the individual states. What ensued was one of the most spirited and contentious debates about democracy in American history.

Three American leaders decided to publish a series of rapid-fire essays—anonymously—to rebut criticism of the document and whip up public support. The authors were Alexander Hamilton, James Madison, and John Jay, and they chose to disguise their identities under a single pen name, Publius. These essays collectively became known as the *Federalist Papers*. Aside from helping to make the case for the Constitution, they are regarded as among the most incisive elucidations of the American political system.

Why did they disguise their names? First of all, two of them were convention delegates in Philadelphia and wanted to hide the fact that they had helped author the Constitution. Disclosure would surely have led to charges of bias. Secondly, they were responding to criticisms that had likewise been levied anonymously by other writers. Most importantly, they wanted Americans to focus on the message itself, not on the messenger. The subject matter was too important to let the national conversation sink into a quarrel about the personalities involved. They hid their names, not out of fear of debate, but to further it.

America's Founders could never have imagined today's world, where public mobs are supercharged by social media. Our attention spans have withered, and our national dialogue has been debased by the politics of personal destruction. When someone speaks, the mob attacks the person, and the ideas are left in the rubble. Then the herd moves on to a new controversy. I am no Hamilton, Madison, or Jay by any stretch, but I believe their example is instructive in our time. At a moment when our nation is again at a crossroads, we need meaningful political discourse that goes beyond the number of followers someone has or the volume of snark they can squeeze into a 140-character message to make it go viral.

I have decided to publish this anonymously because this debate is not about me. It is about *us*. It is about how we want the presidency to reflect our country, and that is where the discussion should center. Some will call this "cowardice." My feelings are not hurt by the accusation.

Nor am I unprepared to attach my name to criticism of President Trump. I may do so, in due course. But when the sitting president prefers to focus on distractions, we need to focus on his character and his record. Removing my identity from the equation deprives him of an opportunity to create a distraction. What will he do when there is no person to attack, only an idea?

So for now, if asked, I will strenuously deny I am the author of this book, including when the president demands we each disavow it. What's more, my descriptions of the president and this administration have been carefully written to prevent any inadvertent disclosure. This text includes an array of firsthand accounts, including some provided by officials other than me. Certain details have been withheld or modified without changing the facts in order to preserve the anonymity of those involved. I may also refer to myself in the third person, where needed. As a result, anyone whose sole purpose in reading this book is to uncover names, including my own, will find they are wasting their time.

This is not about eminence. I am not seeking the spotlight or to burnish my reputation. That is why I published my views anonymously in the first place, with the hope of focusing attention on the substance. Sadly, when this is released, little can be done to keep the conversation in Washington from devolving into a contemptible parlor game to guess the identity of the author. Outside of the Beltway, however, I believe Americans are starved for a real discussion going into the 2020 election about the qualities that are requisite for a president. If so, they have come to the right place.

To be clear, I have not written this to settle scores. My primary focus is the president of the United States, not taking shots at my colleagues by peddling a "tell all" narrative of Washington intrigue. I have deliberately limited my descriptions of fellow senior officials, and where possible I have avoided discussing their actions and opinions by name. This town has been corrupted by a slash-and-burn culture, where people tell stories through the press meant to cut others down while building themselves up. This is one of the many symptoms of our fraying civic life. I will do my best not to exacerbate it with this book.

My motive is also decidedly *not* financial. When I was told I could earn a seven-figure monetary advance for writing this work, I refused to even consider it. Our republic is at risk, and I'm not seeking to profit from issuing that warning.

Introduction

If there are royalties from the sale of this book, I plan on donating them substantially to nonprofit organizations that focus on government accountability and on supporting those who stand up for the truth in repressive countries around the world.

Here at home, one of the recipient organizations will be the nonpartisan White House Correspondents' Association, whose mission is to ensure a free press and robust coverage of the presidency, as well as to assist the next generation of aspiring reporters through generous scholarships. If in any measure my tenure in public service can help more journalists hold their leaders to account, then something useful will have come of it.

There are many "leaks" from this administration, perhaps more than any before it. While some officials tell stories to reporters to brag, to advance a personal agenda, or to retaliate against others, many appear to be doing so because they are alarmed at what they have seen in this White House. Sources decline to attach their names to these anecdotes out of fear of retribution. The reluctance is not surprising given the president's penchant for using his position to mock, bully, berate, and punish. I have heard his words of warning to administration officials thinking about departing, and I have seen how his supporters torment those who have crossed him, including going after the innocent family members of dissenters.

Donald Trump is fond of telling officials that he learned an important lesson in business: People are not scared when you threaten a lawsuit, but they *are* scared when you actually sue them. That is among his favored methods of argument—attacking critics to intimidate and silence them. He has been doing it for years.

After I published the op-ed in the *Times*, Trump responded with a one-word tweet: "TREASON?" Those seven letters say it all. To the president, criticism is treasonous. I find this to be a very un-American position. Former president Theodore Roosevelt argued that it was treacherous *not* to criticize the nation's chief executive, as long as it was honest criticism. "To announce that there must be no criticism of the President, or that we are to stand by the President, right or wrong, is not only unpatriotic and servile, but is morally treasonable to the American public," he wrote. "Nothing but the truth should be spoken about him or anyone else. But it is even more important to tell the truth, pleasant or unpleasant, about him than about anyone else." We do not owe the president our silence. We owe him the truth.

It is worth noting that there is a difference

between legitimate criticism and the careless release of sensitive information. Roosevelt said it was "unpatriotic not to tell the truth" about the president, except "in the rare cases where this would make known to the enemy information of military value which would otherwise be unknown to him." In other words, national security information must be protected. I agree. There have been instances in which, on matters of great sensitivity, the current president has failed the American people by making poorly reasoned decisions, whether in the White House Situation Room or in sensitive conversations with foreign leaders. Some of these examples have been declassified, which we will discuss. Those which haven't will not be the subject of this book and such details have been omitted. When individuals leak classified information to the press even to make a valid political critique, it can put Americans in danger. Such disclosures should rightfully be condemned and have no place in our public discourse. There are appropriate avenues for whistleblowers to raise classified concerns, which some have already done.

At the same time, it is equally unacceptable for a president to conflate personal criticism with a national security threat. In summer 2018, he ordered staff to revoke the security clearances of former intelligence officials who disagreed with him, and he directed the White House press secretary to announce that the credentials of former CIA director John Brennan, a frequent administration critic, would in fact be rescinded. What would we have said if his predecessor, President Barack Obama, had done the same? Only a few weeks later, in reference to the op-ed, he demanded that "the Times must, for National Security purposes, turn him/her [the author] over to the government at once!" Trump went further and launched a search effort using taxpayer dollars and official government resources to draw up a short list of people considered potential suspects, before the effort fizzled out for lack of leads. It was Trumpian in every way, a pointless and emotion-driven exercise.

He has suggested worse be done to his critics. In September 2019, the president issued a veiled threat against an intelligence community employee who reported the president for inappropriately coaxing a foreign government to investigate one of his political opponents. Trump said the employee was "close to a spy." He continued, "You know what we used to do in the old days when we were smart, right? The spies and treason, we used to handle it a little differently than we do now." The implicit suggestion was that the whistleblower should be hanged.

Such behavior is unbecoming of a president and the presidency. To anyone with even a modest reverence for the principle of free speech, it is also morally wrong. The nation's chief executive should never under any circumstances use his office and its extraordinary powers to seek revenge against whistleblowers and political opponents. These are actions we would expect from tin-pot dictators in repressive countries and which we would openly decry as a nation. Yet it is happening in real time here at home, setting a chilling precedent for the use of executive authority.

Many were unsure what we were getting when Donald Trump was voted into office for the first time in 2016. Nevertheless, he deserved a chance from all Americans, despite what was said in the campaign or what he'd done at other points in his career. He became *our* president, not just the Republican victor. But now we do know what we've gotten. We all know. This book will illuminate the reality of the Trump administration and whether the current president is fit to continue leading the United States of America.

I write this on the eve of what may be the most important election of our lifetimes. In the time left until we make our decision, we as a nation must consider the implications of reelecting Trump. I realize that writing this while the president is still in office is an extraordinary step. Some will find it disloyal, but too many people have confused loyalty to a man with loyalty to the country. The truth about the president must be spoken, not after Americans have stood in the voting booth to consider whether to give him another term and not after he has departed office. It must be done now. Hopefully others will remedy the error of silence and choose to speak out.

In these pages, you will not just hear from me. You will hear a great deal from Donald Trump directly, for there is no better witness to his character than his own words and no better evidence of the danger he poses than his own conduct.

CHAPTER 1

Collapse of the Steady State

"No government, any more than an individual, will long be respected without being truly respectable; nor be truly respectable without possessing a certain portion of order and stability."

—James Madison

The day began like any other in the Trump administration: with a self-inflicted crisis. It was Wednesday, December 19, 2018, and the White House was dealing with a communications problem. The State Department had decided to unveil an economic development program in Latin America the day before, which experts believed would reduce violence and instability in the region. There was one catch. The president was on the brink of scrapping it. He reportedly thought it was too expensive and threatened to kill the deal by tweet.

Its architects panicked about whether the president was going to create a diplomatic row.

As it often does, the main show turned out to be a sideshow. The president hadn't yet come down from the residence to the Oval Office. We all knew why. It was prime tweeting hour, and at 9:29 a.m., he fired off a missive from the executive mansion: "We have defeated ISIS in Syria, my only reason for being there during the Trump Presidency." Within minutes, news broke that the president had decided to withdraw. He later tweeted: "After historic victories against ISIS, it's time to bring our great young people home!"

The announcement reverberated across Washington. It was contrary to what had been recommended to him. From the top Pentagon officials to leaders of the intelligence community, most of the president's top advisors cautioned against arbitrarily pulling the roughly two thousand US troops out of Syria. ISIS was still a potent threat, he was told, and America's exit would allow the group to reconstitute and plot more deadly attacks. An early pullout would also cede the area to a dictator who used chemical weapons on his own people, to the anti-American Iranian regime that was expanding its reach in the region, and to Russia. What's more, it would probably result in the slaughter of Kurdish forces who had helped us go after terrorists. In every way, withdrawal would damage US security interests.

The president was unmoved. Rather than convene his national security team to discuss options, he bucked them with a tweet.

"People are going to fucking die because of this," a top aide angrily remarked. We all scrambled to figure out what had happened and what Trump's plans were. US allies were baffled and alarmed. The Department of Defense was in the dark. Officials couldn't even figure out how to respond to press inquiries since it was a decision in which they had played virtually no role. The nation's top military brass were infuriated at the lack of pre-planning, as the sudden announcement meant soldiers on the ground could immediately become sitting ducks, potentially vulnerable to attack from opportunistic adversaries who saw them as being in retreat. The military hastily began contingency planning to ensure US forces were not put in harm's way.

We'd all seen presidents make poor decisions when it came to America's defense. This was different. None of us could recall it being done so casually. In a normal White House, decisions of this magnitude receive sober deliberation. They are the subject of sensitive meetings—sometimes too many meetings—just to make sure the details are right. All of the bases get covered, and every question gets answered. How will our enemies interpret this? What can we do to affect their thinking? How will our partners react? Most importantly, how will we best protect the American people, including our men and women in uniform? None of these questions were answered beforehand.

Not only was the decision reckless, but administration officials had been testifying under oath that ISIS was *not* yet eliminated. They also publicly vowed that the United States would *not* abandon the fight in Syria. Now the president was falsely declaring ISIS to be finished, because he just decided it was true one day. He was broadcasting to the enemy that America was headed for the exits. "We are going to get hauled up to the Hill and crucified for this," a senior cabinet member lamented.

In Congress, reaction came swiftly, including from Trump's own party. "I've never seen a decision like this since I've been here in twelve years," a baffled Senator Bob Corker, then chairman of the Senate Foreign Relations Committee, told reporters. "It is hard to imagine that any president would wake up and make this kind of decision, with little communication, with this little preparation." Even Senator Lindsey Graham, who'd been trying to curry Trump's favor, blasted the decision. Lindsey told reporters the announcement had "rattled the world."

It was a watershed moment for another reason, too. It signaled the downfall of key officials who thought they could bring order to the administration's chaos. One in particular decided enough was enough.

The day after the Syria tweets, Secretary of Defense Jim Mattis announced his resignation. In a letter to the president, he wrote: "My views on treating allies with respect and also being clear-eyed about both malign actors and strategic competitors are strongly held and informed by over four decades of immersion in these issues...Because you have a right to have a Secretary of Defense whose views are better aligned with yours on these and other subjects, I believe it is right for me to step down from my position." Mattis set a departure date of February 28. Jim Mattis is a patriot and war fighter who had earned bipartisan support when he was nominated for secretary of defense. Perpetually stoic, he'd told senators concerned about Trump that he wouldn't for a moment sit idle if he felt the president was asking him to do

things that ran contrary to his conscience or that
would needlessly put lives in danger. Jim was, as
ever, true to his word. The resignation shook the
White House, all the way into the Oval Office.

The press called it a protest resignation. President Trump was incensed. In classic fashion, one
bad decision led to another. Within days, the president decided in a temper tantrum to move Secretary Mattis's departure date forward. He wanted
Jim out as soon as possible. This once again threw
the Department of Defense into unnecessary turmoil, as aides scrambled to figure out the succession
plan. Leadership changes atop the world's mighti-
est military usually take several months to game
out to ensure stability. Trump chopped it down to
a few days. He tweeted that the Pentagon's number two would assume the duties of the top job on
January 1, two months sooner than planned. The
next week, in the Orwellian up-is-down culture
that we'd all grown accustomed to, the president
bragged that he "essentially" fired the decorated
marine general. The loss was felt throughout the
administration and the world. One of the few reasonable hands on board the ship of state was headed
overboard.

From the very start, like-minded appointees
observed the president's erratic management style

with concern. We made a concerted effort to replace the tumultuous environment with a disciplined policy process—in other words, a system for making sure presidential decisions were considered thoughtfully, procedures were followed, all sides of a debate were considered, and ultimately that the president was set up for success, including with advisors willing to speak up when the president was headed in the wrong direction.

We thought the situation was manageable. We were dead wrong. If 2017 marked the rise of a loose cabal of pragmatists in the Trump administration—a "Steady State"—2018 marked the start of its demise.

State of Chaos

The early days of any presidential administration are tough. You can't hand over the reins of a $4-trillion-a-year organization, with millions of employees, and expect a seamless transition. The outgoing White House typically directs agencies to help prepare their replacements to take over. Leading up to the inauguration, a flurry of briefings are held, new employees are informed about sensitive programs, and memos are prepared to bring the incoming team up to speed. Sometimes an outgoing administration will offer to leave some of their own officials in place for a few weeks or months into the new president's term in order to make the hand-off easier. Even then, it's still never enough to prepare any group of people for the extraordinary challenge of running the United States government.

For the incoming Trump administration, the situation was much harder.

It's all been spun differently now, but few people on the Trump campaign—up to and including the candidate himself—truly expected to win. It showed. The mood was bleak for employees of his transition team, the group of aides responsible for mapping out an "administration-in-waiting" in the event that Trump won. Some were sending out résumés to find work before the voters of Pennsylvania, Michigan, and Wisconsin cast historic ballots on November 8.

The election result left the transition team rattled, now that they were actually going to be in charge of a presidential transition. Inexperienced operatives admitted they were not ready. Most had never led a government changeover, and they were left without the guidance of seasoned veterans from previous Republican transitions, many of whom had decided to sit the race out, certain there would be no Trump presidency. What remained was a bench of B-listers. Nonetheless, the head of Trump's transition team, New Jersey governor Chris Christie, believed he had a plan, albeit with a staff lagging behind in preparations when compared to its predecessors. Those designs ended up on the ash heap of history, as did their designer. Fresh off his election victory, President-Elect Trump suddenly decided to sack Christie as the transition chief and make Vice-President-Elect Pence the new chair. The hasty move set the incoming administration back weeks in some ways, if not months.

Abraham Lincoln famously constructed a "team of rivals" after he won office, assembling his former competitors into a cohesive cabinet. But because of poor planning and widespread doubt about his prospects, Trump wound up with the opposite: "rival teams." Infighting from the campaign spilled over into the presidential transition. Advisors brandished their knives, back-stabbing each other to get the jobs they wanted. At the same time, a parade of job-seekers made the pilgrimage to Trump Tower in New York to pay homage to the incoming commander in chief, seeking a place on his short list. Most had conveniently changed their minds about the president-elect. Factions formed. Conspiracies to undermine potential candidates—while boosting others—were hatched and dissolved, sometimes in the same day. There was the Kushner camp, the Bannon camp, the Conway camp, and others such as Penceland or the so-called Flynn-stones, acolytes of the anointed national security advisor. They were united at times and divided at others. This was a real-life version of *The Apprentice*. Some of these rivalries persisted deep into the start of the president's term. Trump often encouraged disunity by making suggestions about who had his favor and who did not.

Despite the internal bedlam, the president-elect did not end up with a government solely populated by flunkies. Far from it, in fact. Although a long list of highly experienced Republican leaders were de-facto barred from the incoming administration for being "Never-Trumpers," those who didn't sign their names onto anti-Trump screeds, myself included, had a shot. Respected political figures and experts signed up. Notwithstanding the surrealness of it all, the process produced a White House team and a cabinet more competent than critics were willing to give Trump credit for. There were former governors such as Nikki Haley and Rick Perry, four-star generals such as John Kelly and Jim Mattis, corporate executives such as Rex Tillerson and Steven Mnuchin, US senators such as Jeff Sessions and Dan Coats, and former cabinet secretaries such as Elaine Chao. This was a solid group of lieutenants for any president-elect and, for a time, Donald Trump's choices were encouraging to those who doubted him.

The assemblage of outsiders helped tamp down some of the feuding within the Trump team. These people had no reason to fight with one another. They were not tainted by the internal politics of the campaign. Unlike the president-elect's friends and the leftovers he brought with him, who were used to currying Trump's favor and surviving his fickle turns of affection, these experienced leaders were not worn down by life inside Trump's inner circle of flattery and deception. The administration's recruits came together because many had one trait in common: They didn't know the chief executive.

False optimism infected the new team. Everyone was hopeful the rancor of the campaign would be replaced by the high purpose of leading the country, which can ennoble even the most distracted minds. "Hope" evaporated on first contact with the president-elect. He was so focused on his "win" that he could barely focus on the forthcoming task of governing. Trump carried around maps outlining his electoral victory, which he would pull out at odd times in discussions meant to focus on preparing him to take office. He would beckon his guests, as well as aides, advisors, and incoming cabinet officers, to gaze at the sea of red on the map, visual proof that he'd won. "Yeah, we know you won," we would think to ourselves. "That's why we're here."

It was clear something wasn't right. Incoming staff exchanged worried glances about what they were seeing during the transition. This place was already crazy, they confided in each other, and Trump hadn't even entered the White House yet. His turbulent demeanor and off-the-wall comments—like his continued fixation with Barack Obama and Hillary Clinton, who were *leaving* government—were not part of a television persona. They were the real thing. His management of the upstart operation was, well, not really management at all.

The bonds that eventually became an informal "Steady State" were tightened not long after the president's inauguration. Only days into office, he invited congressional leaders to the White House to meet. This was supposed to be a bipartisan show of goodwill. But at the outset of the meeting the president railed against what he claimed were "millions" of people who voted illegally in the election, depriving him of winning the popular vote. The assertion had been debunked previously, and it was so clearly false on its face that no one could believe he was raising it again. After the meeting, we tried to brush it off by joking that the president was off his rocker. But it wasn't really a joke. We were genuinely worried by the tone he was setting. Then there were his actions.

President Trump signed off on a rapid-fire barrage of executive orders intended to undo Obama administration policies, cut regulations, spur economic growth, and more. On the surface, everyone agreed with the goals. Only a few aides had been involved in the drafting, though, and the president didn't really seem aware of what he'd done. Some orders were so hastily written that they backfired spectacularly, like the president's travel ban on citizens from supposedly terrorist countries—an order that wound up in the courts, was publicly protested, and needlessly cost the administration early congressional and public goodwill. New White House appointees and agency officials were livid that the rollouts weren't more carefully planned.

Then the president decided to give his chief political strategist, Steve Bannon, a seat on the National Security Council (NSC). This really got folks up in arms. The NSC is a White House organization responsible for advising the president on the most sensitive matters of intelligence, defense, and diplomacy that affect the lives and safety of Americans at home and around the world. Seats at the table are typically reserved for top agency heads, not media advisors. NSC matters weren't supposed to be "political" discussions. In this case, Bannon was elevated, while others, such as the chairman of the Joint Chiefs of Staff and the director of National Intelligence, were effectively demoted. The president's most experienced recruits were astounded. Although Trump reversed the order a few months later, it wasn't forgotten.

The administration was only a few weeks in, and already the mayhem made everyone look foolish. Internal whispers grew louder: This was not a way to do business. As a result, people who'd previously been outsiders to Trump World grew closer to one another and developed a bizarre sense of fraternity, like bank-robbery hostages lying on the floor at gunpoint, unable to sound the alarm but aware that everyone else was stricken with the same fear of the unknown.

"He's About to Do Something"

To be clear, there is no seditious plot inside the administration to undercut the president. The

Steady State is not code for a coordinated scheme to sabotage his policies or, worse, oust him from office. I use "resistance" in quotes because it's neither the Right's fear of a "Deep State" gone rogue, or the Left's conception of an active subversion campaign. Trump's critics, who are rooting for an actual resistance, have let their imaginations run wild with the idea of public servants frustrating the gears of government to bring down Trump. If this kind of conspiracy exists, it's news to me, and it would be disturbing. Public service is a public trust. Any government employee with such a nefarious end goal should be condemned.

Instead, the early Steady State formed to keep the wheels from coming off the White House wagon. When presidential appointees started conferring about their shared concerns with the nation's chief executive, it was not in dimly lit, smoke-filled back rooms of Washington. It was done informally, in weekly phone calls or on the margins of meetings. People who compared notes during the workday and in the normal course of business realized that the administration's problems were more than fleeting. They were systemic. They emanated from the top.

Two traits are illustrative of what brought the Steady State together: the president's inattentiveness and his impulsiveness. Both will be documented further in this book. But coming to terms with these characteristics for the first time had a powerful impact on the people serving in the administration.

Take, for instance, the process of briefing the president of the United States, which is an experience that no description can fully capture. In any administration, advisors would rightfully want to be prepared for such a moment. This is the most powerful person on earth we are talking about. But before a conversation with him, you want to make sure you've got your main points lined up and a crisp agenda ready to present. You are about to discuss weighty matters, sometimes life-and-death matters, with the leader of the free world. A moment of utmost sobriety and purpose. The process does not unfold that way in the Trump administration. Briefings with Donald Trump are of an entirely different nature. Early on, briefers were told not to send lengthy documents. Trump wouldn't read them. Nor should they bring summaries to the Oval Office. If they must bring paper, then PowerPoint was preferred because he is a visual learner. Okay, that's fine, many thought to themselves, leaders like to absorb information in different ways.

Then officials were told that PowerPoint decks needed to be slimmed down. The president couldn't digest too many slides. He needed more images to keep his interest—and fewer words. Then they were told to cut back the overall message (on complicated issues such as military readiness or the federal budget) to just three main points. Eh, that was still too much. Soon, West Wing aides were exchanging "best practices" for success in the Oval Office. The most salient advice? Forget the three points. Come in with one main point and repeat it—over and over again, even if the president inevitably goes off on tangents—until he gets it. Just keep steering the subject back to it. ONE point. Just that one point. Because you cannot focus the commander in chief's attention on more than one goddamned thing over the course of a meeting, okay?

Some officials refused to believe this is how it worked. "Are you serious?" they asked, quizzing others who'd already briefed the president. How could they dumb down their work to this level? They were facilitating presidential decisions on major issues, not debates about where to go out for dinner. I saw a number of appointees as they dismissed the advice of the wisened hands and went in to see President Trump, prepared for robust policy discussion on momentous national topics, and a peppery give-and-take. They invariably paid the price.

"What the fuck is this?" the president would shout, looking at a document one of them handed him. "These are just words. A bunch of words. It doesn't mean anything." Sometimes he would throw the papers back on the table. He definitely wouldn't read them.

One of the hardest culture shifts took place with the National Security Council. NSC staff were accustomed to producing long-winded classified memos. But if the aim was to educate *this* new commander in chief, they couldn't submit a fifty-page report entitled something like "Integrated National Strategy for Indo-Pacific Partnership and Defense," expect him to read it, and then discuss it. That would be like speaking Aramaic to Trump through a pillow; even if he tried very hard to pay attention, which he didn't, he wouldn't be able to understand what the hell he was hearing.

It took a lot of trial and error for West Wing staff to realize there needed to be a change in the White House briefing process. Until that happened, officials would walk out of briefings frustrated. "He is the most distracted person I've ever met," one of the president's security lieutenants confessed. "He has no fucking clue what we are talking about!"

More changes were ordered to cater to Trump's peculiarities. Documents were dramatically downsized, and position papers became sound bites. As a result, complex proposals were reduced to a single page (or ideally a paragraph) and translated into Trump's "winners and losers" tone.

Others discovered that if they walked into the Oval Office with a simple graphic that Trump liked, it would more than do the trick. We might hear about it for days, in fact. He would hold on to the picture, waving it around at us in meetings. "Did you see this? Can you believe this? This is beautiful. Something truly special. Dan!" He might summon the White House's social media guru, who sits just outside the Oval Office. "Let's tweet this out, okay? Here's what I want to say…" That way the public would get to share in his excitement, too.

One graphic that left Trump spellbound was intended to explain certain government and industrial relationships. The basic depiction of interlocked gears, likely pulled from clip art, showed how different elements of the government bureaucracy depended on parts of the private sector. The president was so mesmerized that he showed it off to Oval Office visitors for no apparent reason, leaving us—and them—scratching our heads. Another time he became enamored with a parody poster in the style of *Game of Thrones*, with the words "Sanctions Are Coming," overlaid on a photo of the president. This was meant to be a teaser for forthcoming Iran sanctions. Trump was elated and tweeted the image out to his followers at once, resulting in a cycle of memes mocking the graphic.

Seeing this type of behavior was both educating and jarring to the burgeoning Steady State. It was a visceral lesson that we weren't just appointees of the president. We were glorified government babysitters.

The feeling of unease was cemented by having to deal with the president's penchant for making major decisions with little forethought or discussion. These "five-alarm fire drills," as I call them, seemed like a curse. When Trump wanted to do something, aides might only get a few hours' notice from him before he announced it. They then launched a frenetic response effort, a race against the clock to reshape his views before the tweet went out. This could upend entire workdays. Over time, the last-minute warnings actually came to be seen as a luxury. It's better to have a few hours—or minutes, for that matter—to intervene than have *no* opportunity at all to convince Trump to hit the brakes on a wacky or destructive idea. He's less inclined to preview his decisions today.

Here is how it might play out in the early days of the administration: The president sees something on television. He doesn't like it. It makes him think, "Maybe I should fire the secretary of commerce," or "We should pull out of that treaty. It's really a terrible treaty, after all." He might tee up a tweet. Then he bounces it off of the next aide he talks to, who is stunned to discover that the terrible idea is tip-of-brain for the president of the United States, and might be on the brink of becoming reality. The aide finds the president disinterested in thinking through the consequences. "We're going to do this today, okay? Tell Sean to get ready." He wants Press Secretary Sean Spicer prepared to defend it to the death.

Staff throw up the Bat-Signal, calling a snap meeting or a teleconference. "He's about to do something," one warns the group, explaining what the president is about to announce.

"He *can't* do this. We'll all look like idiots, and he'll get murdered for it in the press," another exclaims.

"Yeah, well, I'm telling you he's going to do it unless someone gets to him fast," the first warns. "Can you cancel your afternoon?"

Officials rush back to the White House. The delicate Oval Office schedule is shattered to make way for an unexpected intervention, and top agency executives scrap meetings with foreign leaders, press conferences, and briefings to join the gathering. The conversation with the president is tense. He wants to do what he wants to do, consequences be damned. It isn't beneath him to attack his own family members, too. "Jared, you don't know what you're talking about, okay? I mean seriously. You don't know." After some dire warnings ("Everyone will get subpoenaed"—"This will cost you dearly with working-class voters"—"This will put Americans in harm's way"), he might show signs of reconsidering. Refusing to admit error, the president insists he still wants to go with his original plan, but he backs off temporarily or agrees to a less drastic measure, averting disaster for the moment.

These mini crises didn't happen once or twice at the administration's outset. They became the norm, a semi-regular occurrence with aftershocks that could be felt for days. Some aides grew so worn down by the roller coaster of presidential whims that they started encouraging him to hold more campaign rallies, putting aside the fact that it wasn't campaign season. The events had the dual benefit of giving Trump something "fun" to do and also getting him out of town, where he would hypothetically do less damage. More public events were put on his schedule, allowing frayed nerves back in Washington the chance to recover.

Yet even when the president was convinced *not* to do something spontaneous and given a few days' distance from the idea, he would still bring it back up when he got back to town. That's the storyline of many of the anecdotes referenced in this book. It might be a desire to fire someone who'd only recently been confirmed by the Senate, like his Federal Reserve chairman, or an itch to issue an executive order to end a deal he hates, like the North American Free Trade Agreement (NAFTA). His cyclical urges can't be suppressed for long.

Steady Staters felt this was becoming a seesaw presidency.

The Broken Branch

Whether you were "all in" on the president's agenda or not, one reality couldn't be denied—lurching from one spontaneous decision to another was more than a distraction. The day-to-day management of the executive branch was falling apart before our eyes. Trump was all over the place. He was like a twelve-year-old in an air traffic control tower, pushing the buttons of government indiscriminately, indifferent to the planes skidding across the runway and the flights frantically diverting away from the airport. This was not how it was supposed to be.

Every White House in recent history instituted a deliberate process by which decisions were made and executed. Policies were carefully considered, final decisions were carried out with a step-by-step plan, partners at other levels of government were rarely caught off guard by White House positions, the paperwork and information the president received was properly vetted and fact-checked, and someone was in charge of overseeing hiring and firing. Family members were kept at a safe distance, and in cases where they participated in governing, like Bobby Kennedy, most had clearly defined roles. Great deference was given to ethics officials and the White House counsel's office, who acted as watchdogs against inappropriate activities by members of the presidential staff. This was all undertaken to ensure the presidency was operating within or sometimes to the limit of its constitutional authorities and in compliance with federal laws. Not in the Trump administration. This approach was abandoned through inattention, intention, incompetence, or all three.

Fundamentally, the president never learned to manage the government's day-to-day functions, or showed any real interest in doing so. This remains a problem. He doesn't know how the executive branch works. As a consequence, he doesn't know how to lead it. The policymaking process has suffered considerably. On any given issue—say, how to fix health care—there is daily confusion between departments and agencies about what the plan is and who is in charge. He tells the secretary of defense to do things that are the responsibility of the secretary of state. He tells the attorney general to do things that are the job of the director of National Intelligence. Sometimes he tells his son-in-law, Jared Kushner, to do all of their jobs at once, including reimagining care for America's veterans, negotiating Middle East peace, spearheading criminal justice reform, and undertaking delicate conversations with foreign allies.

Jared is a likable person, a youthful and energetic advisor and an empathetic listener. However, when the secretary of defense is cut out of Jared's meetings regarding a crucial part of the world, or the national security advisor isn't back-briefed on an important conversation Kushner has with a foreign ambassador, it can cause problems, sometimes big problems. It isn't clear the president is satisfied that so many issues run through his son-in-law's office, but the arrangement persists because Jared is careful to always demonstrate loyalty to his wife's father, even at the expense of his standing among other top officials. Thus, the unclear and unhealthy lanes of authority persist.

The White House, quite simply, is broken. Policies are rarely coordinated or thoroughly considered. Major issues are neglected until a crisis develops. Because there is no consistent process, it is easy for the administration to run afoul of federal laws, ethics guidelines, and other norms of behavior. We will walk through a fraction of the mind-numbing examples in this book, but it will take many years to fully capture the scope of the unruliness.

There is no shortage of people, inside and outside the administration, who want to convince you and themselves that this is an act of three-dimensional chess. Trump is doing all of this for a reason. Just wait and see. It's part of his genius. During the administration's infancy, a handful of aides went as far as to argue that management-through-chaos was an asset. Among them was Stephen Miller, a senior advisor to the president and early campaign hand Trump inherited from Jeff Sessions. He is a hard-liner who developed a name for himself in certain Washington circles with his preachy warnings about illegal aliens and for filibustering on these themes in conversation. A cunning aide who relishes having the president wrapped around his finger on any number of issues, Miller back-channels his side of the story to the press, and works daily to outwit other aides who sit just down the hall from him. Like Jared, he is careful not to show daylight between himself and the president, for fear of losing his stature as a Trump whisperer.

Stephen has argued that Donald Trump's impulses needed to be encouraged, not tempered. From the beginning, he agitated for the White House to "flood the zone" by issuing as many dramatic policy changes as possible, regardless of whether they would withstand legal scrutiny. It would shock the system and put "the opposition" (Democrats) on their heels, he contended. It would also create powerful distractions the White House could exploit, drawing fire away from the real policies hard-liners cared about. To Stephen, chaos is a deliberate governing strategy.

He is not alone in the misguided view. A now former top aide was fond of comparing the president to General George S. Patton. Contemporaries could never predict what Patton was going to say or do. "That's how I like it," General Patton is said to have remarked. He wanted to keep everyone, especially the enemy, on their toes. "That is the political genius of Trump," the aide reminded us during a heated debate over a particularly troublesome presidential decision. "He is just like Patton." The argument might have some merit, if the president displayed any sense that he knew what he was doing.

The Steady State grew more worried about the condition of the executive branch. The Patton approach doesn't work in a democracy. It's okay to leave foreign enemies on a battlefield confused about what you are planning, but not the American people or the Congress or your friends and allies. Officials decided they didn't want the president's willingness to play fast and loose with the powers of government to trickle down to lower levels of the bureaucracy, where they could infect the culture. Department and agency heads started insulating their operations from Trump's whims and created separate discussion forums run outside of the White House. They confessed wariness about sending staff to the West Wing for meetings, not wanting more junior officials to see how bad it was or partake in the gross mismanagement.

It was getting ugly. As the old saying goes, this was no way to run a railroad. In fact, if railroads were run this way, trains would go in the wrong direction, or never show up at all, or crash into each other. The conductor would be unqualified, the engineer would be fired in the middle of a trip, and Chinese-built trains would zip right by us, watching the disaster with wonder at their unbelievable good fortune.

Putting out Fires

"Among us friends, let's be honest," a prominent presidential advisor once remarked, after the pro-chaos crowd left a White House meeting. The slimmed-down group was comprised of White House officials and cabinet secretaries. "About a third of the things the president wants us to do are flat-out stupid. Another third would be impossible to implement and wouldn't even solve the problem. And a third of them would be flat-out illegal." Heads nodded.

That day, the group was gathered to discuss a presidential proposal that fell into the first category. Trump wasn't halfway through year one, and he wanted to shut down the government because he was unhappy with congressional budget negotiations. He'd been talking about it behind closed doors for weeks. Now he was bringing it up in press conferences and tweeted that the government needed a "good shutdown." The president certainly had the constitutional right to do it. He could veto whatever spending bill was sent to his desk. But it was bound to be a political loser. Federal employees would be without pay, essential services would abruptly halt, and in the end we knew the Democrats were prepared to dig in harder. Picking this fight, advisors warned, could cost the party congressional seats in next year's midterm election.

We tipped off Republican leaders in Congress that they needed to take it seriously. The president wasn't just playing a game. "He's crazy as a lunatic," one West Wing advisor told the Speaker's office. Paul Ryan's team was exasperated and urged us to just "take the win" because they'd already gotten concessions from the Democrats in budget talks. Staff arranged for Trump to hear from Republican members of Congress. They warned him that he would be putting the party's majority in jeopardy if he caused a shutdown at the end of the fiscal year. They helped persuade him that we would lose the fight and that it wasn't worth it. The president reluctantly agreed and stood down.

For now, the Steady State had put out the fire, a duty that became an all-consuming function despite the day jobs we'd been hired for. But of course President Trump would revisit the idea of a government shutdown later on, seeking a different outcome.

In the second category—things that the president asks for that "would be impossible to implement and wouldn't even solve the problem"—we found ourselves tamping down requests from the impractical to the disturbing.

Take February 2018, for instance, when the president proposed a way to end gun violence in our schools. He suggested to aides that weapons be given to all of America's teachers so they could fight back against mass shooters. This was typical Trump. An idea was formed in the ether of his mind, and he decided it was brilliant because he thought of it. Most sane folks raised an eyebrow. The teachers we remembered tended to be gentler souls like Betty White, not Annie Oakley. We wanted to hand Betty and all of her colleagues a pistol? When this idea seemed unpalatable to us, he ratcheted it back to 20 percent of educators—a figure that seems to have just popped into his head. With 3.7 million teachers in the United States, that would still mean training or putting guns in the hands of nearly a million of them. As Steady Staters tried to explain, this would be wildly impractical and would undoubtedly make the gun violence situation more contentious.

The president took the idea public anyway. "So let's say you had 20 percent of your teaching force, because that's pretty much the number," Trump said, describing the plan. "If you had a teacher who was adept at firearms, they could very well end the attack very quickly." It was time for all of us to reenact the daily face-palm ritual. It wasn't that everyone thought having armed and trained officials in schools was bad, it's just that the president had no conception of what was doable and what was nuts.

One Harvard gun violence expert summed up the public reaction: "It's a crazy proposal. So what should we do about reducing airline hijacking? Give all the passengers guns as they walk on?"

Fortunately, the idea was dropped because no one else took it seriously, much like the president's claim that he would be the citizen-hero if he was on the scene of a school massacre. "I really believe I'd run in there, even if I didn't have a weapon," he claimed. We couldn't contain our laughter.

Most concerning are the one-third of "things the president wants us to do [that] would be flat-out illegal." In fairness, when Trump suggests doing something unlawful, it's not necessarily nefarious. More often than not, it's because he doesn't understand the limits of federal law. He might order an agency to stop spending money on something he dislikes, not knowing he generally can't cut off funds Congress has already approved. For instance, Trump has repeatedly tried to stop the flow of aid to countries overseas, complaining we are wasting money that should be spent at home. His demands began within weeks of taking office and only got worse when he got briefed about US activities in places such as Africa and Southeast Asia to fight deadly diseases or to invest in activities that are designed to protect US economic interests. "Why the hell are we spending so much money there?" he'd demand, directing officials to stop the programs altogether, which of course they couldn't do. They'd explain to him that only Congress could make those cuts. He'd say he didn't care and to do it anyway, but then he'd appear to drop it for the time being. In other cases he thought of the funds as bargaining chips, as in the case of money earmarked by Congress to go to Ukraine, and tried to pause the funds for whatever purpose suited him at the moment, perhaps until he got something he wanted in return.

Or he might tell one of his departments to take an action the law explicitly forbids. This happens a lot with acquisitions. The president inserts himself regularly into discussions about Pentagon purchases, forgetting that the US government isn't like the private sector, where he can pick a favorite contractor based on personal preferences. He memorably came into office determined to negotiate costs down for the next-generation Air Force One (which he claimed he successfully accomplished, though that's actually not what happened). To prevent corrupt practices, agreements for the purchase of new aircraft or defense technologies often must be advertised and bid competitively, with strict selection criteria. The president can't just jump into the fray and pick his favorite company. Once these limitations are explained to him for the umpteenth time, he'll usually (begrudgingly) relent.

"The president will let me do whatever the hell I want," a newly minted cabinet secretary remarked after receiving an inappropriate request from Trump. Walking out of the West Wing, he paused and turned around, adding, "That's why I have to take this job extra seriously." The president doesn't police bad behavior in his cabinet, he encourages it. Aides have to self-police.

Other presidential orders cannot be written off to ignorance. This dilemma occurs frequently on the hot-button issue of immigration. The president gets animated on the subject, to say the least, and somehow it's become a part of all of our lives, even when it's not in our respective portfolios. Almost anything, any issue, and problem can be tied back to immigration in his mind.

At one point, Trump warmed to a new idea for solving what he viewed as the biggest crisis in American history: to label migrants as "enemy combatants." Keep in mind this is the same designation given to hardcore terrorist suspects. If we said these illegals were a national security threat, Trump reasoned, then the administration had an excuse to keep all of them out of the country. It was unclear if someone had planted this in his head or whether he had come up with it on his own, but either way, advisors were mortified.

Trump toyed with the shocking proposal in meetings having nothing to do with the subject, asking random advisors what they thought. Word got around. It's times like these when people freeze and don't know what to say. They'll give him one of those polite smiles reserved for a deranged relative who thinks you want to hear about his soul-searching solo retreat to the Rockies. Not receiving too much resistance, Trump went further and mused about shipping the migrants to Guantanamo Bay, where hardened terrorists were jailed. In his mind, the deterrent would be a powerful one: Come to the United States illegally, and you will be sent to a remote US detention facility in Cuba to live alongside murderous criminals.

The rumor escaped the confines of the White House. "Are you fucking kidding me?" one career State Department official blurted when informed of the proposal. "This is completely batshit." Advisors worked to shut it down quickly and quietly. They argued it was wildly impractical (how could you ship thousands of migrants a day to Cuba?) and too expensive (Trump often was persuaded against something if he thought it was too pricey, ironic for someone who is driving the country deeply into debt). Left unsaid was the more obvious reason. It was truly insane, on its face, for America to send migrant children and families to a terrorist prison in Cuba.

Finally, aside from its ineffectiveness and moral offensiveness, the policy would be outright illegal. Migrants seeking shelter in the United States are not "enemy combatants." They are not engaged in hostilities against the United States on behalf of foreign states or terror groups, even though the president and his border agencies like to insinuate that the throngs of arriving migrants could have dangerous militants in their midst. Rational people know that the vast majority are innocent people trying to get to America for a better life. Despite the president's recurring desire to do so, the law cannot be shaped like Play-Doh and made to say whatever he wants it to say. Before the president could make a public case for the concept, officials quashed it.

Or did they? That's the question with any of the above ideas. You never really know if the fire has been put out completely. There may still be hot embers. Glimpses of them will appear in press conferences and off-the-cuff presidential statements. Then, one afternoon, the blaze might come roaring back, such as Trump's recurring demands for one-on-one meetings with the world's most brutal dictators. On some days, the return of a half-baked suggestion is harmless. On other days, it would cost the president his office if it was carried out. Ironically, many of those who worked to protect the president from losing his job became some of the people he was most interested in firing.

Dismantling the Guardrails

Donald Trump built his reality television career on the image of a tough boss. The immortal words "you're fired!" became associated with Trump himself, establishing a unique place in the public lexicon. The president relishes this image and brought it with him into the White House. He keeps officials on their toes by wondering aloud about their tenure within his administration. He fans the flames of gossip about potential firings, often starting the rumors himself by complaining about his aides, knowing listeners will spread the word.

Officials are perpetually on "deathwatch," as it is known inside the administration, waiting for that assassination tweet to come. Every week there is a new potential victim. For a president known for demanding loyalty pledges, this is a pernicious way of making sure staff do what he wants, by reminding them that the ax could come down at any time.

He publicly teased the possibility of firings after the midterm elections. "I have a fantastic cabinet," he told reporters when asked about a shake-up, but added, "There are a few positions I am thinking about...I could leave it the way things are now and be very happy with it, or make changes and maybe be even happier with those positions." Trump let some of the names leak into the press. Really, he wanted everyone to be concerned they were in the crosshairs.

No one is immune, including those he has known for years. One day, Treasury secretary Steven Mnuchin was the target of presidential ire for failing to follow through on an impossible task Trump assigned to him. The president wanted Mnuchin to use his powers to levy a new tax on certain types of financial transactions. The secretary explained repeatedly why he couldn't do what was being demanded, but Trump complained behind his back.

"Every time I ask Mnuchin about this, he's got another excuse. 'We can't do this, we can't do that,'" he said, half faking the voice of Mnuchin, a man he has known for close to two decades. "What good is he? I thought we had the right guy at Treasury. But now I don't know. Maybe not so much. What do you think—personnel mistake?" He likes to poll the room when someone is on the ropes. People laugh or offer approving facial expressions, usually relieved that the anvil isn't hovering over their own head.

Trump will leave people in the lurch for weeks, months, or longer. He notoriously kept Kirstjen Nielsen, his homeland security chief, flummoxed about whether and when she might get sacked. For Director of National Intelligence Dan Coats, his time in limbo was far longer. Rumors trickled out periodically for years that the president was dissatisfied and might be considering a change. The West Wing corner office that belongs to the national security advisor appears to be the most cursed, as all of its occupants under Trump have dealt with regular speculation from down the hall about whether their time has come.

The president considered making changes to the top of the ticket, too. On more than one occasion, Trump has discussed with staff the possibility of dropping Vice President Pence in advance of the 2020 election. Although Mr. Pence has been loyal to a fault, the president is always eager to "shake things up," and Trump's view of loyalty, of course, is self-serving to the extreme. Former UN ambassador Nikki Haley was under active consideration to step in as vice president, which she did not discourage at first. Some of Trump's closest advisors have suggested she would help shore up the president's unpopularity with women, which demonstrates how little this White House understands women in the first place.

Trump avoids directly firing people, contrary to his television image. Instead he takes the cowardly way out and cuts them loose by way of social media. In July of 2017, he got rid of his first chief of staff, Reince Priebus, with a tweet. Priebus expected to be removed and personally offered to resign, but he didn't know his canning was imminent. After returning from a trip to New York, the president tweeted out, "I am pleased to inform you that I have just named General/Secretary John F. Kelly as White House chief of staff. He is a great American..." Reince was sitting yards away in the presidential motorcade in the rain when he got the news. The president had not yet departed Air Force One. Another humiliating spectacle.

Incredibly, the first official duty of the new chief of staff was to get rid of someone else the president wouldn't fire himself, Anthony Scaramucci, the short-lived White House communications director. The day he was sworn in, John Kelly told Scaramucci his eleven-day tenure was finished. It wouldn't be the last time he'd have to deliver bad news that Trump wouldn't.

Kelly's ascent to the White House was generally met with optimism, albeit with pockets of trepidation from those who sensed he wasn't as politically astute as others on the team. Regardless, officials prayed for a new sense of order. They got it for a time. Access to the president was more tightly controlled, preventing unnecessary distractions. The day became more structured. The new chief of staff was also willing to be frank with the president when Trump lurched toward a bad decision. As a result, the anxiety level went down a few notches, and a false sense of security set in.

Kelly also tried to curb ad-hoc decision making and spontaneous presidential directives. John told agency heads he was establishing a system to make sure the president heard all sides of a debate so he could make informed choices. That usually required pleading for time with the commander in chief so that a subject could be considered at lower levels of government and fleshed out into a set of sensible options.

Afghanistan was a prime example. Donald Trump announced before his presidency that the United States should pull out of this "total disaster" and "endless" war. Once in office, he didn't seem interested in contrary opinions. Security officials feared that pulling out suddenly would plunge Afghanistan back into chaos, and they urged him not to make a wartime decision right away. They persuaded him to wait. In the meantime, a process was put in place to develop options, which were battle-tested by the national security team.

Toward the end of the summer, a special Camp David retreat was organized to walk the president through the proposals. Trump was starting to allow Kelly to manage the process—and to manage him. The results were atypical. The team laid out the pros and cons of each option over the course of an hours-long discussion. Trump asked tough questions, and he got nuanced answers. The conversation was mostly cool-headed, organized, and rational. It was everything other decisions hadn't been. In the end, the president agreed to a more thoughtful strategy focused on a long-term solution, rather than immediate withdrawal or capitulation to the murderous Taliban regime. Steady Staters silently declared victory. Maybe the administration could be stabilized after all.

Of course, as we all feared, the newfound sense of order didn't last long. Trump grew to despise the insinuation that he needed to be managed at all and began circumventing the new structures that had been put in place. As spring 2018 rolled around, the president agitated for additional personnel changes in his still-young administration. Top advisors were forced to spend inordinate time persuading the president not to fire fellow members of his team, usually the ones who were more comfortable telling him "No." Over time, a feeling of insecurity returned to the administration, and the Steady State recognized that Trump's demeanor couldn't be moderated.

It got harder and harder to convince the president to avoid reckless decisions. Improving the "process" wasn't a durable solution. It was just a wet Band-Aid that wouldn't hold together a gaping wound. We realized as year two wore on that we couldn't rely on any system to instill in the president the leadership traits he'd never developed. We returned to running interference against gross impulsivity, confronting each third-rate presidential contrivance as it came and trying to make the best of it.

Senior advisors and cabinet-level officials pondered a mass resignation, a "midnight self-massacre," as noted earlier, to draw the public's attention to the disarray. At any given time during the Trump administration, there are at least a handful of top aides on the brink of resigning, either out of principle or exhaustion. Several departure timelines appeared to be converging in 2018, creating the possibility for a simultaneous walkout to prove our point about the president's faltering administration. Every time this was contemplated, it was rejected. The move was deemed too risky because it would shake public confidence and destabilize an already teetering government. We also didn't want to litter the executive branch with vacancies. Maybe, we thought, it could still get better. It didn't. It went downhill, and the vacancies followed anyway.

Disaffected officials were picked off by the president, one by one. Trump is adept at identifying anyone with an independent streak who might challenge him. Others departed of their own accord. The ranks of experienced leaders started thinning fast. Economic advisor Gary Cohn announced his resignation shortly after the one-year mark. Then the president fired Secretary of State Rex Tillerson. Then he forced out national security advisor H. R. McMaster, followed by homeland security advisor Tom Bossert. Then UN ambassador Nikki Haley said she was resigning. Then the president fired Attorney General Jeff Sessions. Then he announced that John Kelly would be out the door soon. Then Jim Mattis resigned. And with the New Year approaching, more heads were reported to be on the chopping block.

As 2018 came to a close, the president could scarcely find a replacement chief of staff. Trump was in crisis mode when his first and only choice for the job, Pence aide Nick Ayers, declined. Once Ayers was out, Trump turned to Chris Christie. After Christie showed disinterest, Trump finally settled on budget director Mick Mulvaney, but only in an "acting" capacity. Such is life in the Trump White House that what is usually the most coveted and powerful staff job in Washington cannot be reliably filled and, when it is, only by a temporary figure. Smart candidates know that the president's whims become his chief's life, and the person is never really in charge. Trump's children are his chiefs of staff. Random Fox News hosts are his chiefs of staff. Everyone is the chief of staff but the chief of staff. It's no wonder people aren't jumping at the opportunity.

The high rate of turnover was a direct result of the president's leadership. He ejected people who were willing to stand up to him. He got bored with officials who weren't dynamic enough or didn't defend him on television. Some escaped the administration because of policy differences, and still others departed to avoid what they perceived to be an inevitably sinking ship. For certain people, it was a combination of all of these factors. John Bolton, Trump's third national security advisor, saved the president many times from irresponsible decisions but grew weary of the turbulence and Trump's fumbling in foreign policy. He resigned of his own volition, but the president still tried to make it look like a firing.

Trump is not bothered by an administration strewn with vacancies. In fact, he says, it's good to have "acting" officials in the top slots. "My 'actings' are doing really great," he told reporters. "I sort of like 'acting.' It gives me more flexibility. Do you understand that? I like 'acting.' So we have a few that are 'acting.' We have a great, great cabinet." Translation: Acting officials are less inclined to ask questions and more inclined to do what they are told. This best explains the slow but systematic purge of the Steady State. With the guardrails disappearing, the road ahead looked all the more ominous.

"God grant that men of principle be our principal men," Thomas Jefferson once wrote.

Good people are needed in government to administer our laws. But the Founders did not want us to put our faith in them exclusively. Public servants are corruptible and expendable. As we will discuss later, that's why the Founders proposed a system of checks and balances, so that negative human impulses would be ameliorated and the power of one branch would be kept in line by another.

Awful ideas are seeping out of the White House at high volume with the ranks of the clear-eyed depleted. Fewer people speak up these days in meetings, and increasingly the voices in Donald Trump's ear are only those who tell him what he wants to hear. If ever there was a victim of confirmation bias—the tendency to search for information that validates one's preexisting beliefs, even if they are wrong—it is him. The danger is that President Trump runs the most powerful government on earth and cannot afford to be without dissenting opinions. Yet the Oval Office has become an echo chamber.

I was wrong about the "quiet resistance" inside the Trump administration. Unelected bureaucrats and cabinet appointees were never going to steer Donald Trump in the right direction in the long run, or refine his malignant management style. He is who he is. Americans should not take comfort in knowing whether there are so-called adults in the room. We are not bulwarks against the president and shouldn't be counted upon to keep him in check. That is not our job. That is the job of the voters and their elected representatives.

Americans' faith in the executive branch should be measured by their faith in the president himself and him alone, not by functionaries in his administration whose names never appeared on the ballot. So that begs the question: *Who is he?*

CHAPTER 2

The Character of a Man

"A good moral character is the first essential in a man...It is therefore highly important that you should endeavor not only to be learned but virtuous."

—George Washington

Everywhere you look within the walls of the White House are shrines to our democracy. On one end of the main floor, George Washington's commanding portrait hangs in the East Room for all to see. First Lady Dolley Madison famously rescued this national treasure before the British set fire to the building during the War of 1812. On the other end, guests are greeted in the State Dining Room by Abraham Lincoln's likeness hanging above the fireplace, one of the most valuable paintings of the sixteenth president. The stately rooms in between, famously restored and redesigned by Jacqueline Kennedy, are filled with priceless artwork, furniture, and symbols of our history.

Upstairs is the president's private residence, where every commander in chief since John Adams has lived with his family. Notable guests stay in the Lincoln Bedroom, which the martyred president once used as a working office, or the Queen's Bedroom, where Winston Churchill rested during wartime visits to Washington. On the ground floor, special guests can tour the White House library, the China Room, the Map Room used by President Roosevelt to monitor sensitive developments during the Second World War, and the Diplomatic Reception Room, where acclaimed world figures have been welcomed to our nation's capital.

Most interest is usually reserved for one room in particular. To get there, you walk out of the White House residence to a building next door: the West Wing. Built in the early 1900s to accommodate a growing staff, the West Wing houses the offices of the president and senior advisors, the Situation Room, the Cabinet Room, and more. The Oval Office is its crown jewel. Itself a historic splendor, the room is iconic, from the presidential seal carved into the ceiling to the Resolute desk, a gift from Queen Victoria in 1880 made from the timbers of a salvaged ship. It is the same desk where Harry Truman displayed a plaque that read "The buck stops here" and where John F. Kennedy's young children sometimes played while their father worked.

The Oval Office fills visitors with a sense of respect. This is where our leaders make life-and-death decisions, shape the direction of our country, and address the people. Ronald Reagan spoke from behind the Resolute desk after the Space Shuttle *Challenger* explosion in 1986, honoring the memory of those lost. "We will never forget them," he said, "nor the last time we saw them, this morning, as they prepared for their journey and waved goodbye and 'slipped the surly bonds of earth' to 'touch the face of God.'" George W. Bush calmed a grieving nation after the terrorist attacks of September 11, 2001, telling Americans from the same room that "a great people has been moved to defend a great nation...the brightest beacon for freedom and opportunity in the world, and no one will keep that light from shining." Whether you are there for a tour, or whether you work for the president, it is hard to shake this quiet feeling of reverence, no matter how many times you enter the room.

That is, until the silence is broken.

"It's a hellhole, okay? They don't let you say 'shithole' anymore. But that place is a hellhole and everybody knows it."

"Watch them start to choke like dogs."

"This place is kind of sexy, isn't it?"

"I don't fucking care. Ooh ooh 'excuses, excuses.' Just stick it to them. I promise you, they will be kissing our asses afterwards."

"I'm hotter than I was then, okay? Because you know you also cool off, right? You do. But I'm much hotter."

"It is very unfair to me. And it's presidential harassment frankly. You can't harass a president."

"Sweetie, your face looked very tired on television. Have you lost weight?"

"I think I've done more than any other first-term president ever."

"If you're going to cough, please leave the room…Do you agree with the cough?"

"I think it's probably, uh, I want them to think whatever they think, they do say, I mean, I've seen and I've read and I've heard, and I did have one very brief meeting on it. But people are saying they're seeing UFOs, do I believe it? Not particularly."

"We have the worst laws and the stupidest judges."

"This guy, have you seen him? 'My Pillow.' He's unbelievable. He buys all the airtime on TV. It's terrific. And he's a big, big Trump supporter."

"This is one of the great inventions of all times—TiVo."

"You're saying it's MY fault? It's all fucked, and it's your fault."

These are the sounds bouncing off those rounded walls today, or on any given day of the Trump presidency. Some of these have been said with television cameras in the room and others with the doors closed. All of them reflect the real Donald Trump. Not everyone sees the full Trump, especially the one who is red-faced, consumed with fury, and teetering at the outer limits of self-control. Visitors are sometimes greeted with something they don't expect.

Many people, including those with a low opinion of the president, tend to be pleasantly surprised when they first encounter him in this place. They don't mind that he has no filter. In fact, there is something refreshing, even charming, about a politician just saying whatever pops into his or her head. He can also be funny. Sometimes he will delight in calling up officials on speakerphone and making jokes at their expense to the amusement of staff sitting on the couches. When so many politicians cling to clichés and talking points, one who is routinely straightforward and indiscreet is kind of disarming.

Those who want to see the best in President Trump, as we tried to do when the administration began, can write off his unorthodox behavior and strange stream-of-consciousness commentary as the result of putting a "disruptor" in the White House. Besides, we used to tell ourselves, there have been a number of chief executives who've acted unscrupulously in office. If those Oval walls could talk, they would recount Lyndon Johnson's vulgar comments and crude advances, John Kennedy's and Bill Clinton's assorted trysts, and Richard Nixon's efforts to obstruct justice and seek vengeance against his enemies.

Trust me, though. This is not the same. In the history of American democracy, we have had undisciplined presidents. We have had incurious presidents. We have had inexperienced presidents. We have had amoral presidents. Rarely if ever before have we had them all at once. Donald Trump is not like his predecessors, everyone knows that. But his vices are more alarming than amusing. Any entertainment derived from seeing this sort of irreverent behavior in the West Wing quickly wears off and is replaced by lingering dread about what comment, tweet, or direct order might come next.

The character of a president should be of the utmost concern for citizens. We are ceding day-to-day control of the government to that person, after all. Along with it, we are delegating decisions that affect our children's futures and our personal well-being. That is why it's every American's responsibility to assess the occupant of the Oval Office and consider the leader's disposition and moral qualities, especially when deciding whether that person remains suited for the role. Before we look at any other aspect of Trump's presidency, this is what we must do.

To judge a person's character, we first must know *what* it is, *how* to measure it, and ultimately *why* it matters.

Defining Character

The debate about character is a philosophical one, specifically a branch of philosophy known as "ethics." Ethics is the study of how a person should act, particularly toward others. That is where character comes in. People have written volumes on the subject and how it should be defined, but you know it when you see it. A person of character is someone who is upstanding, who is reliable, who carries him- or herself with dignity. A basic definition says character is "the mental and moral qualities distinctive to an individual," but it's not enough to *have* good morals. Your behavior must spring from them. Simply put, your moral code is your "software"—your belief system—that operates your "hardware"—your body and its actions.

The important question when looking at a president is: *What should those moral qualities be? What are the ideal traits we expect a leader to demonstrate?*

The question of character consumed the Ancient Greeks. Their greatest philosophers, including Socrates, Plato, and Aristotle, all asked themselves, "What makes a man 'good'?" A rough consensus emerged about core elements. These qualities came to be known as the "cardinal virtues": wisdom, temperance, courage, and justice. They were deemed to be the behaviors a person needed in order to reach high moral standing.

A few hundred years later, another thinker took these virtues a step further. Cicero, a revered Roman luminary, was interested in more than just a man's character. He wanted to explore a *statesman's* character. The Roman Republic was in crisis, overrun with arrogant and dishonorable men, so Cicero decided to examine what moral qualities were needed in great leaders. Influenced by the philosophers before him, he wrote a seminal work, *De Officiis* (or "On Duties"). In the form of a letter addressed to his son, Cicero spelled out how a public servant should behave. His tome has since inspired great figures throughout world history, including America's Founding Fathers.

What does this have to do with Donald Trump? Well, Cicero gave us a useful guide for measuring a leader's character. His four-part rubric will sound familiar: (1) "understanding and acknowledging truth"; (2) "maintaining good fellowship with men, giving to every one his due, and keeping faith in contracts and promises"; (3) "greatness and strength of a lofty and unconquered mind"; and (4) "the order and measure that constitute moderation and temperance." In short, it was a version of the cardinal virtues—wisdom, justice, courage, and temperance. His formula is as relevant in today's fractured political climate as it was during the rockiest days of the Roman Republic, which is why we are going to use it to assess the current president.

Before we inspect Trump's character, we need to ask ourselves whether it matters at all. As I said, the United States has been led by men who displayed less-than-model behavior during their presidencies, to put it mildly. They cheated on their wives and the public. They broke their promises. Yet these executives still managed to accomplish admirable

81

feats to advance civil rights, spur economic growth, and defend the country against foreign enemies. Can't Trump still do great deeds without being a man of impeccable character? If Trump is flawed, or deeply flawed, does it really make a difference?

The answer to both questions is "yes."

Great deeds can be done by imperfect men. We just need to decide whether it's worth it. Unscrupulous presidents have been successful at times, but it came at a cost. Was it worth it to elect James Buchanan, for example, a president who delayed the nation from plunging into civil war, but only by defending the institution of slavery and protecting the slave-holding interests of the South? In hindsight, most would say no. He should have had the spine and grit to confront the scourge of slavery. Buchanan is now considered to be one of the worst American presidents.

Our leaders don't need to be superheroes. Most are far from it. However, we should invest in someone whose virtues *outweigh* their vices. A president must be equipped to do more good than harm for the people. His or her character may not inform every single decision, but it will shape their overall record, which is important because we depend on our president for a lot. We rely on the president to manage the largest enterprise in the world, the US government; to lead the nation through crises, whether it's a natural disaster or an attack; and to set an agenda to move the country forward. Finally, we rely on the president to be a role model. Those who are exalted get emulated. When we put the chief executive on a pedestal, young people in particular will learn from the leader's behavior, setting the tone for future civic engagement.

A man's character is tested when he's given power. That much we know from history. President Trump has been in power for several years, and he's been thoroughly tested. The results are revealing. It's been said that character is a tree, and reputation its shadow. The character of the president casts a long shadow across all Americans, and in time, his reputation will become our own. As you read this chapter ask yourself: *Is this who we are? If not, is this who we want to be?*

The President's Wisdom

When I contemplate President Trump's "wisdom," I'm not talking about encyclopedic knowledge. Cicero said true wisdom doesn't require knowing all the facts up front. Rather, it consists of "learning the truth," an eagerness to seek the facts and to get to the root of an issue. He warned it is wrong to claim to know something you don't, or to waste time on frivolous issues. It is "dishonorable to stumble, to wander, to be ignorant, and to be deceived." In other words, a leader should not fall for "fake news" and assume something is true when it's not.

Does Donald Trump possess these essential characteristics of wisdom?

Let's start with a curious mind. Trump doesn't have a deep bench of knowledge about how government works. He's never served in it, and he'd never run for any office prior to the 2016 campaign. It would be unfair to expect him to understand all the nuances of the legislative process or how a large bureaucracy functions. What is troubling about the president is not that he came into office with so little information about how it runs. It's that he's done so little to try to learn more in order to do his job.

Donald Trump is not a curious person. He barely reads, if at all, and he scolds officials who come to brief him with anything more than the most succinct reading material possible, as noted previously. "It's worse than you can imagine," former economic advisor Gary Cohn reportedly wrote in an email. "Trump won't read anything— not one-page memos, not the brief policy papers, nothing. He gets up halfway through meetings with world leaders because he is bored."

During the campaign, candidate Trump variably touted and dismissed his own reading habits. He proclaimed himself a great advocate of the Bible, remarking in February 2016 that "Nobody reads the Bible more than me." He was unable to point to a single Bible verse that he found inspiring, almost certainly because he's never actually read it. I've never heard him mention scripture of his own accord, nor has anyone else I know. When pressed further about his reading habits, Trump once said he had no time to dive into books. "I never have. I'm always busy doing a lot." At one point, news host Megyn Kelly asked him about the last book he read, to which Trump responded, "I read passages. I read areas, chapters. I don't have the time. When was the last time I watched a baseball game?"

The lack-of-time argument is dubious. Looking each morning at the president's daily schedule, any of us could tell you he carves out more than enough time to do what he wants. The demands of the job rarely keep him away from the golf course. Both of President Trump's predecessors, Bush and Obama, were voracious readers. Trump himself frequently stays up late in the residence, and he often doesn't start the day in the Oval Office until 10 or 11 a.m. Rather than consume books, he spends his time bingeing on cable news, tweeting, and making phone calls. In his own words, Trump says he doesn't need to read to make informed decisions because he acts "with very little knowledge other than the knowledge I [already have], plus the words 'common sense,' because I have a lot of common sense and I have a lot of business ability."

The sheer level of intellectual laziness is astounding. I found myself bewildered how anyone could have run a private company on the empty mental tank President Trump relies upon every day to run the government. On television, a CEO-turned-showman can sit around a desk and bark orders at subordinates and then go to commercial. In real life, a successful CEO has to absorb a lot of information, about the economic climate, about his or her competitors, about product and consumer trends. How can you manage a sprawling organization if you won't read anything? Not very well, it turns out.

The president does *claim* to be highly intelligent, though. He has been touting his intellect for years and loves to boast about his great brain in private meetings at the White House. In 2013, he tweeted: "Sorry losers and haters, but my I.Q. is one of the highest—and you all know it! Please don't feel so stupid or insecure, it's not your fault." In 2016, when asked during the campaign whom he was consulting on foreign policy, he responded: "I'm speaking with myself, number one, because I have a very good brain, and I've said a lot of things…My primary consultant is myself, and I have, you know, I have a good instinct for this stuff." On the contrary, outside advisors who helped him with debate prep were mortified by his lack of understanding on the subject. In 2018, he took to Twitter again to burnish his cognitive credentials: "My two greatest assets have been mental stability and being, like, really smart," he posted in January 2018. "I went from VERY successful businessman, to top T.V. Star…to President of the United States (on my first try). I think that would qualify as not smart, but genius…and a very stable genius at that!" Intelligence is one of those qualities that, if you insist you have it, you probably don't. Nonetheless, Trump is known to interrupt briefings with assertions along the lines of, "Yeah, I get it. I'm pretty smart, okay?"

The president frequently claims to be an expert on issues about which, in reality, advisors will have found out he knows very little. Here is a sample from a much larger list put together by astute observers:

On campaign finance: "I think nobody knows more about campaign finance than I do, because I'm the biggest contributor."

On the courts: "I know more about courts than any human being on Earth."

On trade: "Nobody knows more about trade than me."

On taxes: "Nobody knows more about taxes than I do."

On ISIS: "I know more about ISIS than the generals do."

On the US government: "Nobody knows the system better than I do."

On technology: "Technology—nobody knows more about technology than me."

On drone technology, specifically: "I know more about drones than anybody. I know about every form of safety that you can have."

On the contrary, I've seen the president fall flat on his face when trying to speak intelligently about most of these topics. You can see why behind closed doors his own top officials deride him as an "idiot" and a "moron" with the understanding of a "fifth or sixth grader." Folks have been forced to publicly deny those specific quotes, usually with non-denial denials. These are the tamest descriptions used internally to express exasperation with the commander in chief. People normally tack a string of expletives onto the front and back ends of their assessments.

You don't always get this level of candor. Even in private, officials are afraid to express their opinions about the president because they don't know whom to trust. In one instance when we were all on the road, a high-level aide waited until we were thirty thousand feet in the air, everyone around us was asleep, and we were out of the country to share his own daily anecdotes of how alarmingly uninformed the president was. The man was a wreck, he lamented, and had a juvenile view of complex subjects. Trump was all over the map when he spoke and was unfocused when it came time to sit down and talk about serious issues. I assured him that was the general experience.

Trump defenders will be tempted to write these off as the musings of Never-Trumpers, but that is not the case. We are talking about people who came into office committed to serving the commander *and* carrying out the mission. I am not qualified to diagnose the president's mental acuity. All I can tell you is that normal people who spend any time with Donald Trump are uncomfortable by what they witness. He stumbles, slurs, gets confused, is easily irritated, and has trouble synthesizing information, not occasionally but with regularity. Those who would claim otherwise are lying to themselves or to the country.

A Warning

The president also can't remember what he's said or been told. Americans are used to him denying words that have come out of his mouth. Sometimes this is to avoid responsibility. Often, it appears Trump genuinely doesn't remember important facts. The forgetfulness was on display after the president was briefed on a major Category 5 hurricane approaching Florida. "I'm not sure I've ever even heard of a Category 5...I don't know that I've ever even heard the term," he told reporters. White House aides were baffled. He'd been briefed on four other Category 5 hurricanes during his time in office. Was he forgetting these briefings? Or more problematic, was he not paying attention at all? These are events that affect millions of Americans, yet they don't seem to stick in his brain.

You don't need to be a presidential appointee to witness his irregular mental state. Just watch any Trump rally. While giving a speech on energy production one day, the president made an errant comment about Japan, complaining that they "send us thousands and thousands—millions!—of cars, [and] we send them wheat. Wheat! That's not a good deal. And they don't even want our wheat. They do it to make us feel that we're okay, you know, they do it to make us feel good." Ignoring the fact that trade with Japan was irrelevant to the speech, the comment didn't make sense. Wheat is not a top US export to Japan. It's not even one of our main *agricultural* exports to the Asian nation, as appointees in our Commerce Department later pointed out. Also, his characterization isn't a coherent way of thinking about how countries purchase goods. Nations don't buy our products on behalf of their people, and they don't do it to make us "feel good." Trump makes such statements *all the time*, leading to our next point.

The president flunks Cicero's "fake news" test badly. The Roman philosopher says it is dishonorable to stumble ignorantly when it comes to the facts and to be deceived. Sadly, Trump has built a reputation on disinformation. Before he was elected, he was a regular booster of Alex Jones, the conspiracy theorist behind the website Infowars. "Your reputation is amazing," Trump affectionately told Jones in one appearance on his show. This, of course, is the same Alex Jones who suggested that the Sandy Hook elementary school shooting was faked and that the Apollo 11 moon landing never happened.

Trump was also one of the most visible adherents of "birtherism," perpetuating (false) suspicion that Barack Obama was not born in America and fearmongering that he'd lied about his religion.

"He doesn't have a birth certificate," Trump told Laura Ingraham in a 2011 interview, "or if he does, there's something on that certificate that is very bad for him. Now, somebody told me—and I have no idea if this is bad for him or not, but perhaps it would be—that where it says 'religion,' it might have 'Muslim.' And if you're a Muslim, you don't change your religion, by the way."

Among many other conspiracy theories, Trump suggested without evidence that Senator Ted Cruz's dad was involved in the Kennedy assassination, that Justice Antonin Scalia may have been murdered, that MSNBC host Joe Scarborough might have been involved in a former intern's death, that a former Clinton advisor's suicide could have been something more nefarious, that Muslim Americans near New York City celebrated in the streets after 9/11, that vaccines cause autism, and more. External observers can barely keep these lists of his claims updated. Internal observers are no better off. We wonder, does he actually believe these conspiracies? Does he just say this stuff to get attention? I can't get into his head, but my guess is a little bit of both.

Serious people throughout the White House cringe when they hear him raise these subjects. Trump will wrap his arms around bogus claims like they are old friends, and he doesn't care if the person spewing them is a fraud, as long as their words serve whatever purpose Trump has in mind at the moment. One of his favorite sources for news analysis is Lou Dobbs, a once-respected Fox host whose late-night show is now riddled with conspiracy theories and wild speculation about current events. The president goes to bed with Lou's ideas floating in his mind, whether it's conjecture about liberal billionaire George Soros or ideas for new Justice Department investigations. We know this because he regularly brings Lou's ideas into the Oval Office the next morning, demanding they be implemented the way Lou said they should be. I can't think of another elected leader in this country who is so easily lured in by obvious carnival barkers.

The president spreads false claims almost daily. He is the nation's most prominent re-tweeter of "fake news" while simultaneously being its biggest critic. In fairness, every president gets facts wrong once in a while. The difference is that those presidents seemed to care when they misspoke. They didn't recite sham information every day as a matter of course without regard for the consequences. Yet after making a demonstrably untrue statement, the president displays zero remorse that he has done so. He's comfortable being a huckster of half-truths.

Both his appointees and the public hear misleading statements from the president so often that we've become desensitized to them, from an early claim that his inauguration was the largest-attended in history (this was easily debunked) to his insistence that the special counsel's report exonerates him (it explicitly does not). We will explore the president's tenuous relationship with the truth in more detail. For now, though, we can safely say that Trump doesn't meet Cicero's standard for someone who reveres and seeks the truth, someone who isn't easily deceived or doesn't spread misinformation.

A wise man he is not.

The President's Sense of Justice

When I refer to "justice," it's not about law and order. Cicero defined the concept as a way of characterizing how an individual treats others. Does the person maintain good fellowship with other people? Does he or she give everyone what they deserve? And does the individual keep faith in contracts and promises? These are the qualities of a "just" person. Cicero adds to the mix that this type of person also displays "beneficence and liberality," i.e., they are kind and generous.

Donald Trump certainly thinks a lot about justice. So much so, in fact, that the president has tweeted about something being "fair" or "unfair" nearly two hundred times since taking office. His concern tends to be about whether he is being treated fairly personally. "Nothing funny about tired Saturday Night Live on Fake News NBC!" he tweeted after the show mocked a White House press conference in February 2019. "Question is, how do the Networks get away with these total Republican hit jobs without retribution? Likewise for many other shows? Very unfair and should be looked into. This is the real Collusion!" The president was insinuating that television networks needed to be investigated and punished for poking fun at him. Thankfully no one was dumb enough to follow up with the Federal Communications Commission to put them on the case.

He spends a lot of time talking to staff about perceived injustices. Trump will complain about his coverage, his critics, and anything else that he believes is unfair. Then he will send White House aides on an endless quest to "fix it." The president might want an aide to get on the phone to scold a television commentator who's been disagreeing with him or to tell a foreign leader that we're "done" dealing with their country because Trump doesn't like what they've said about a White House policy. It's gotten so tiring that aides will acknowledge the gripe and pledge to remedy it, while letting it drop to the very bottom of (or off) their to-do lists because the problem is impossible to fix, pointless to address, or requires a counterproductive solution.

No venue is off limits for his complaints of injustice. Shortly after assuming the duties of commander in chief, Trump traveled to Central Intelligence Agency headquarters to speak to America's covert workforce. His remarks were bookended with complaints about unfair news coverage. "As you know, I have a running war with the media," he told the audience. "They are the most dishonest human beings on Earth." All of us watching it winced. The president was making his comments in the most inappropriate setting, not just because he was at the CIA, but because he was standing in front of the agency's memorial wall for fallen officers. President Trump did the same four months later in front of hundreds of US Coast Guard Academy cadets, turning part of their commencement ceremony into a rant about the press. "Look at the way I've been treated lately!" he remarked, going off script and shaking his head. "No politician in history—and I say this with great surety—has been treated worse or more unfairly."

When it comes to his treatment of others, it's difficult to say the president meets Cicero's criteria. In fact, Trump is better described as "ruthless" than "just." This is not solely my assessment. It's his own self-perception. "When someone attacks me, I always attack back…except 100x more," he tweeted in 2012, describing his attitude of unequal retribution as "a way of life." Trump echoed the sentiment in his book *The Art of the Deal*, writing that when he believes he is being treated unfairly, "my general attitude, all my life, has been to fight back very hard."

Trump's hit-hard philosophy is not reserved for those who have legitimately wronged him. The president picks fights indiscriminately. The volume of examples is breathtaking. Look no further than his Twitter account on any given week, or a short digest of the news. One moment he might be attacking soccer star Megan Rapinoe, and the next he is mocking the prime minister of Denmark, Mette Frederiksen. Other times, he is assailing his own top officials.

The attacks on his hand-picked chairman of the Federal Reserve, Jerome Powell, are a recurring example. Trump regularly launches unprovoked broadsides against Powell and his independent agency, which the president is frustrated that he doesn't control. In separate Twitter outbursts, Trump suggested the Federal Reserve chairman "cannot 'mentally' keep up" with central banks in other countries and asked followers which was a "bigger enemy" of the United States, Powell or China's dictator? All of this because Powell's agency has been candid about economic indicators that show the president's policies have been risky.

Giving nicknames to his targets is a favored tactic, too, allowing the president to turn attacks into instant memes. He road tests the insulting monikers with friends and is elated he has a new one to give to Dan, the social media aide. There's Da Nang Dick (Senator Dick Blumenthal), Pocahontas (Senator Elizabeth Warren), Low Energy Jeb (former governor Jeb Bush), Slimeball (Jim Comey), MS-13 Lover (Speaker Nancy Pelosi), Dumb as a Rock Mika (MSNBC's Mika Brzezinski), the Dumbest Man on Television (CNN's Don Lemon), and so on. Often Trump hones in on physical features, using names like Fat Jerry (Representative Jerry Nadler), Little Marco (Senator Marco Rubio), and Dumbo (for his former Secret Service director). Other acid-tongued presidents have had words for people they didn't like, but I can't think of any who regularly went out of their way to humiliate people with childish nicknames. If there is any silver lining, its that he typically keeps the R-rated ones within the West Wing.

There are no two ways about it. Trump is a bully. By intimidating others, he believes he can get what he wants, not what is fair. It's a philosophy he brags about. He regales staff with stories about filing meritless claims in court against other companies in order to coerce them to back down or to get a better deal. That's how you get them to do what you want. During the 2016 campaign, journalist Bob Woodward asked Trump about President Obama's view that "real power means you can get what you want without exerting violence." In his response, Trump made a revealing confession: "Real power is through respect. Real power is, I don't even want to use the word, fear."

President Trump shows no mercy. Political opponents are wartime opponents, and there should be no clemency. Trump remains fixated on his previous presidential rival years into his tenure, continuously disparaging and demeaning her. It might be a different situation if he expected to face off again with Hillary Clinton, yet she appears to be finished with public office. Don't get me wrong. No one in the Trump White House is a fan of Hillary Clinton, but we started to find the president's chronic animosity toward her to be a little weird. He has tweeted about Clinton hundreds of times since taking office. He has even flirted with using the powers of his office to investigate and prosecute her, as we will discuss. Electoral defeat is not enough; Donald Trump wants total defeat of his opponents.

Cicero said "justice" is to be measured by whether someone keeps promises, too. Sadly, Trump's past is rife with allegations of stiffed contractors, unpaid employees, broken agreements, and more. An investigation by *USA Today* found he'd been involved in more than 3,500 lawsuits over the span of three decades, many of which included claims by individuals who said he and his companies failed to pay them. His businesses also received repeated citations from the government for violating the Fair Labor Standards Act and failing to pay overtime or minimum wage.

The trail of broken contracts runs parallel to another Trump trait, his lack of generosity. Kindness and liberality are part of Cicero's justice checklist, but they are not a part of Trump's character. His philanthropic history is full of empty words and questionable practices. The president's surrogates claim he has given away "tens of millions" to charity over his career, yet investigations by journalists have found the cash donations to be far less than he boasts.

Most of Trump's charitable giving was apparently done by the Trump Foundation. Rather than fund it himself, the businessman reportedly used outside donors to fill the foundation's coffers, allowing him to write checks with his name on them without diminishing his own wealth. This is not unheard-of. Other personal foundations are boosted by outside donations. But in December 2018, the foundation was forced to dissolve after a state investigation in New York accused it of "a shocking pattern of illegality," including "functioning as little more than a checkbook to serve Trump's business and political interests." In one instance, he used ten thousand dollars in money from his charity to buy a six-foot oil portrait of himself. So much for the spirit of giving. That's not to say Trump doesn't donate his own money. He's made a big show within the White House of his decision to forego the $400,000 presidential salary, periodically giving away his paychecks in grand fashion to highlight his magnanimity. Whether it's at the Department of Transportation or the Surgeon General's Office, he brags about it on Twitter and in person. Trump has gone as far as to insist recipients stage photo ops with the checks—prominently featuring his name, signed in a big Sharpie—to show their gratitude. I don't recall other presidents calling attention to their generosity like this so regularly. You should see the awkward reaction from agency heads who realize they are expected to humbly exalt the president when he throws pocket change their way, after burning through millions in their budgets in ways they wouldn't have recommended under any other president. As one joked to me, at least it's a way for him to pay the taxes he probably owes the American people.

Together, these examples paint a clear picture. Donald Trump is not a paragon of justice. He is not worried about maintaining "good fellowship" with people, treating others fairly, keeping his promises, or demonstrating generosity. While he has sought to cultivate the image of an unselfish billionaire, he is not. Many of us who've joined his administration recognize he is a vindictive and self-promoting person, one who spends inordinate time attacking others to advance his interests. Those qualities translate into governing. As a result, we have all learned the hard way that the president's modus operandi emphasizes combat over peacemaking, bullying over negotiating, malice over clemency, and recognition over true generosity. In sum, he is the portrait of an unjust man.

The President's Courage

Cicero says courage is the "virtue which champions the cause of right." The president believes he is the champion of great, righteous causes. He carries the banner on any number of public issues with his fight-to-win style. A courageous person takes both credit and blame when they are the leader, yet Trump refuses to do the latter. When his team loses, Donald Trump is nowhere to be seen. That's when he shows his true colors. Look at any legislative fight the administration has had with Congress. If we were on the side that failed, the president did everything to avoid blame for fear of being labeled "the loser."

The atmosphere created by his craven attitude is dispiriting to the team. I remember during the president's first year how often he promised we were going to reform the US health care system, a topic of major focus during the campaign. Trump pledged to repeal and replace Obamacare, which was replete with problems and distorting the marketplace. It looked like Republicans had the votes in Congress, but when the effort inexplicably collapsed, the president didn't show courage by taking the fall. He pointed fingers at "weak" senators who voted against repeal and privately blamed staff. Little has happened on the issue since. His "I'm not it" demeanor has been copied by those beneath him, creating a culture where people scurry away from problems to avoid shouldering the blame. Scott Pruitt was remembered for this during his tenure as the head of the Environmental Protection Agency, where he blamed staff for his misuse of government funds rather than take responsibility. He was ultimately forced to resign.

Bravery comes in different forms. It's not just a willingness to take a popularity hit when something doesn't go the right way. It can be far more serious. In some cases, it means actually putting your life on the line. I don't know how many times Trump has been in such a position (most people rarely are in their lives), but the one example we have is telling.

At the height of the Vietnam War, when others were joining the US military to serve their country, he sought to avoid the draft. Trump received five deferments: four for education, one for medical reasons. The excuse? "Bone spurs" in his feet. The injury was concocted, according to the daughters of the podiatrist who made the diagnosis, as well as the president's former lawyer, who recounted Trump saying, "You think I'm stupid? I wasn't going to Vietnam." Don't fool yourself into believing this goes unnoticed by the men and women he commands in the United States military or the veterans who didn't have a convenient way out of Vietnam. They would have gone to war with or without an excuse, and they deserve better than the boasts of a man who stayed home.

Bravery is not the only component of courage, so it is unfair to judge the president on that score alone. Cicero suggests that a courageous person also is someone who is not swayed by the masses—"He who is carried by the foolishness of the ignorant mob should not be counted a great man"—and someone who is not "conquered by pleasure" and greed—"Nothing is more the mark of a mean and petty spirit than to love riches." Fortitude is also important. "It is the mark of a truly brave and constant spirit that one remain unperturbed in difficult times, and when agitated not be thrown, as the saying goes, off one's feet, but rather hold fast to reason, with one's spirit and counsel ready to hand."

Thus, aside from bravery, the checklist for a courageous person includes resistance to the mob mentality, avoidance of obsession with money and pleasure, and stability through crises.

On the first account, it would be difficult to describe the president as someone who is not carried away by public passions. As we will discuss later, he fuels rather than avoids mob behavior. And he is demonstrably obsessed with public opinion. This is second nature to a man who spent years obsessing over TV ratings. Our tweeter in chief survives on a diet of "likes" and "retweets." Analysis of his feed shows that he has mentioned opinion polls almost every single month since becoming president. It's not rare for a meeting about economic growth or national security to include stray comments about recent poll numbers.

His favorite polls are, predictably, any that show him ahead, regardless of how dubious the sourcing. Trump blows his top when outlets report his unpopularity, especially those that he thinks should be in his camp, such as Fox News, when their professional polling operation accurately reflects his unpopularity. Polls and polling to him are demonstrations of loyalty, not scientific measures of the country's mood. They aren't data points to help feed into deliberations, as with any other politician on earth; they are only meant to feed his vanity. If they don't, then they must be wrong. We know where such an attitude inevitably leads—failure. Margaret Thatcher, a giant of modern history to whom Trump could never be favorably compared, once warned, "If you set out to be liked, you would be prepared to compromise on anything at any time, and you would achieve nothing." The president's craving for high approval ratings is ironic, because he does little to deserve them.

As for whether or not he is "conquered" by money and pleasure, I will again let Donald Trump speak for himself:

"I have made the tough decisions, always with an eye toward the bottom line."

"The point is that you can't be too greedy."

"Part of the beauty of me is that I am very rich."

"You have to be wealthy in order to be great."

Trump's love of money is second only to his love of luxury writ large. His expensive personal tastes and extravagant lifestyle are well documented. They were on full display for America his first week in the White House. Days into the administration, Trump used one of his first major interviews as president to brag to the *New York Times* about his new famous home. "I've had people come in; they walk in here and they just want to stare for a long period of time," he said. Trump touted the building's many rooms and priceless artwork, not to mention the impeccable service. He woke up to buffet spreads of fruit, pastries, and treats. The staff stocked all of his favorite snacks. And the phones, he said, were "the most beautiful phones I've ever used in my life." "It's a beautiful residence, it's very elegant," he gushed to the paper.

He reserved his most unintentionally revealing remarks for when the *Times* asked about the Oval Office, which he'd already redecorated with new drapes and a rug. Trump told a story about a recent visitor. "The person came into the Oval Office and started to cry. This is a tough person by the way. But there is something very special about this space," he told the paper. "They see the power of the White House and the Oval Office and they think, 'Yes, Mr. President.' Who tells you no?"

Lastly, Cicero defines courage as the mark of someone who is "unperturbed in difficult times," a quality that I cannot assign to President Trump. When faced with tough challenges, he becomes unglued and bombastic. The fallout isn't always contained within the White House. It explodes weekly into public view. Aides have stopped counting the number of press conferences, interviews, and events that have gone completely sideways because the president is so unmoored by a problem, whether it is a personal spat or negotiation with Congress.

When he is angry about an issue, Trump will let the frustration in his mind boil over, no matter where he's at or what he's doing. It might be the most straightforward event. "Person A will speak," an aide will brief him. "Person B will introduce you, Mr. President. And then you will deliver the following written remarks." She hands him a short speech. Trump will glance at the page, cross the words out with a big black Sharpie, and then take the remarks in a different direction. If the press is in the room, the direction he tends to go is off the deep end of the swimming pool. He'll change the order of events on the spot and launch into a tirade. That's how an event about tax reform can turn into an endless rant about "millions and millions" of illegal voters ruining the democratic process.

When faced with foreign policy dilemmas, his tendency is to puff up his chest and feign toughness, not to keep his cool. For instance, rather than dismiss incendiary adversaries, Trump tries to outdo them: "North Korean Leader Kim Jong Un just stated that the 'Nuclear Button is on his desk at all times.' Will someone from his depleted and food starved regime please inform him that I too have a Nuclear Button, but it is much bigger & more powerful one than his, and my Button works!" In response to Iranian saber-rattling, the president tweeted, "If Iran wants to fight, that will be the official end of Iran. Never threaten the United States again!"

These outbursts might be cathartic in the moment, but they tend to aggravate the situation. Egging on unstable dictators risks a misunderstanding that can spiral into a crisis. At a minimum, the above examples led to prolonged public feuds that distracted from the issue at hand or delayed our ability to respond effectively to international events.

Aristotle once wrote that "he who exceeds in confidence when it comes to frightening things is reckless, and the reckless person is held to be both a boaster and a pretender to courage." Trump is not brave, nor unswayed by the crowd, nor uncommanded by money and pleasure, nor stable through crises. He is a "pretender to courage," and that should give everyone pause.

The President's Temperance

Finally, we must judge Trump's "temperance," which is easier to do than the other virtues, for it is the most obvious. Cicero explains the characteristic as someone showing "restraint" and "modesty," and "being seemly." Said another way: "conducting oneself in an inoffensive manner." Cicero adds that such a person is also not careless. "One must ensure, therefore, that the impulses obey reason...that we do nothing rashly or at random, without consideration or care." He concludes that men of temperance handle criticism well and are not readily provoked.

It should be evident by now that Trump is one of the more offensive public figures in recent times. The president has difficulty showing restraint and lashes out without warning. His behavior is quint-essentially unseemly, from crude rhetoric and vulgar jokes to immodest public reactions. There are far too many examples, so we will choose one category. Nowhere is this more apparent than in his attitude toward women. Many in the Trump administration are put off by his misogynistic behavior, which began well before the election.

How does Trump talk about women? Sex appeal. Beautiful piece of ass. Good shape. Bimbo. Great in bed. A little chubby. Not hot. Crazed. Psycho. Lonely. Fat. Fat ass. Stupid. Nasty woman. Dog. Ugly face. Dogface. Horseface. Disgusting. These are the types of comments he makes. Trump did not spare his opponent—the first female presidential nominee of a major US political party—of his sexism either. "If Hillary Clinton can't satisfy her husband," he tweeted in 2015, "what makes her think she can satisfy America?" At a campaign stop in Ohio the next year he remarked, "Does she look presidential, fellas? Give me a break." I don't care if you supported Hillary Clinton or not. There is no denying the smoldering sexism heaped onto these words.

At times, his sentiments border on what many women today would call predatory. Trump once purportedly made the following statement, referring to himself in the third person: "Love him or hate him, Donald Trump is a man who is certain about what he wants and sets out to get it, no holds barred. Women find his power almost as much of a turn-on as his money." (Here again I can't resist citing Margaret Thatcher, who dealt with men like this: "Power is like being a lady," she remarked. "If you have to tell people you are, you aren't.") In 2013, Trump opined on the tens of thousands of unreported sexual assaults in the US military, tweeting: "What did these geniuses expect when they put men & women together?" And of course, he famously described to NBC's Billy Bush his efforts to win over a married woman and how he approached seduction in general. "I don't even wait," he said. "And when you're a star, they let you do it. You can do anything. Grab them by the pussy. You can do anything."

As president, the inappropriate comments

about women haven't abated. I've sat and listened in uncomfortable silence as he talks about a woman's appearance or performance. He comments on makeup. He makes jokes about weight. He critiques clothing. He questions the toughness of women in and around his orbit. He uses words like "sweetie" and "honey" to address accomplished professionals. This is precisely the way a boss shouldn't act in the work environment. Trump's commentary on specific women in his administration sometimes will happen right in front of them. After one such instance, an official came to me, exasperated, to commiserate. "He is a total misogynist," she complained. "This is not a healthy workplace."

I'm not trying to say women who work for Trump are victims who can't handle themselves. Women have had to deal with creeps long before Donald Trump came into office. They don't need "safe spaces" set up in the West Wing. Still, his displays of misogyny are unusual and unsettling to women who at times feel they are given different treatment than their male counterparts. When it's about female leaders outside the administration—TV hosts or public figures—word gets around about the president's offensive remarks and asides, and we bemoan in private another deep character flaw over which we have no control. Not even his family is off limits, although sharing his last name usually preserves them from the worst, though not the weirdest, comments.

Shifting public attitudes appear to have had little effect on his views toward sexual harassment. Indeed, Donald Trump is like the Fred Flintstone of the "Me Too" era. He's been accused of sexual misconduct by roughly two dozen women, and his strategy is to shred their testaments to his inappropriate behavior. In an exchange between the president and a friend about inappropriate conduct, journalist Bob Woodward recounts Trump saying: "You've got to deny, deny, deny and push back on these women. If you admit to anything and any culpability, then you're dead…You've got to be strong. You've got to be aggressive. You've got to push back hard. You've got to deny anything that's said about you. Never admit." Understood, Mr. President. This quote didn't escape notice by the women on your staff.

Cicero says temperance demands forethought and doing nothing "at random." Yet the president is notorious for his rash decision-making, as discussed throughout this book. Trump boasts of making tough calls based on his "gut instincts" in the moment, rather than good information and a clear strategy.

Then there are the distractions. It's no exaggeration to say we have a commander in chief who is channel-surfing his way through the presidency. Meetings are constantly interrupted by TV. Conversations are sidetracked by commentary about TV. Early morning phone calls are made from the residence about what he saw on TV. He displays fury at what is *not* on TV, including lieutenants who avoid going on cable networks to defend him. Trump takes notice when they skip the Sunday shows or pre-scheduled appearances to avoid having to answer questions about his latest antics, and he holds it against them. The president, as has been amply documented, is obsessed with television, and segments he doesn't like can derail entire workdays across the administration. It's his gluttonous, vanity-pleasing digestion of TV coverage about himself that leads to the most embarrassing outbursts.

I recall one bright Tuesday morning, when the president was still in the residence. A Twitter alert popped up on my phone. Trump was venting about something he'd evidently seen on cable news. In that moment, he could have chosen to talk about the meeting he'd had the day before with the Brazilian president. Or the funerals that were taking place in New Zealand after a mass shooting by a white supremacist. Or the fact that it was his son's birthday. Instead the president was going off on George Conway, the husband of his senior advisor Kellyanne Conway, whose critiques of the president were making minor news.

"George Conway, often referred to as Mr. Kellyanne Conway by those who know him, is VERY jealous of his wife's success & angry that I, with her help, didn't give him the job he so desperately wanted. I barely know him but just take a look, a stone cold LOSER & husband from hell!" Rather than focus on issues that mattered that day, he let Mr. Conway's criticism distract him completely. He redirected the news cycle toward total nonsense. Not to mention the fact that he openly derided the spouse of one of his employees, another workplace red flag.

These flare-ups are constant. They come at the worst times. For instance, on the anniversary of the September 11 attacks, the president couldn't bring himself to hold off on politics for the morning to honor the victims and their families. He lashed out at Democrats and media outlets. "In a hypothetical poll, done by one of the worst pollsters of them all, the Amazon Washington Post/ABC, which predicted I would lose to Crooked Hillary by 15 points (how did that work out?), Sleepy Joe, Pocahontas and virtually all others would beat me in the General election," he tweeted at daybreak. "This is a phony suppression poll, meant to build up their Democrat partners." "Damn it," I thought, "can't we just focus for a few hours?" Other times the White House might be in the midst of responding to a national crisis, but a fly on the wall will find the president is far more interested in responding to "the haters" online than doing his job.

Calm leaders are able to let criticism wash over them. President Lincoln claimed to avoid reading personal attacks altogether. When he *did* encounter a particularly strong critique of his presidency, he would sit at his desk and compose a fiery refutation. After that, he would get up and walk away without sending it. That is not the Trump style. The president takes all criticism personally. He cannot imagine letting it go unanswered. Unlike Lincoln, he does not see temperance as a virtue. He hits "send."

I still remember the gnawing ache in the pit of my stomach. The quiet tension. The sunken faces at work. We were zombies roaming the administration. No words had to be exchanged. The day we all knew was coming had arrived. The day that any remaining questions about President Donald J. Trump's character were definitively answered. For some, it was a turning point. There are many episodes that capture Donald Trump's character, but this one stands out in my memory.

On August 12, 2017, organizers of what was called a "Unite the Right" rally gathered to protest the removal of a Robert E. Lee statue from a park in Charlottesville, Virginia. That was their excuse for getting together, at least. They welcomed well-known white supremacist groups, including neo-Nazi and neo-Confederacy organizations as well as the Ku Klux Klan. The local media covered the lead-up to the rally extensively. On the previous evening, white supremacists conducted an unauthorized march through the University of Virginia campus, where they chanted, "Jews will not replace us," "white lives matter," and "blood and soil." They were met by university students who had stood together around a statue of Thomas Jefferson to oppose the group. The encounter turned violent, only exacerbating the unease in the city before the larger event was scheduled to take place the next day.

A counterprotest to the "Unite the Right" rally was organized, representing a wide swath of religious, ethnic, and other interest groups, as well as concerned local citizens. Violent clashes again followed. In the afternoon, the scene turned deadly. A self-identified white supremacist from Ohio deliberately rammed his vehicle into a crowd of counterprotestors, sending bodies flying into the air. More than thirty people were reported injured, and one woman, Heather Heyer, was killed. The city declared a state of emergency. The crisis in Charlottesville became an international news story.

It is impossible to know exactly what information Donald Trump absorbed about this event, the first real test of his ability as president to respond to civil unrest in our country. He weighed in from his golf course in New Jersey, stating that there was "no place for this kind of violence in America." That was not all. He condemned the hate and "the violence on many sides."

On many sides.

What on earth did he mean by that, I thought, when he uttered the words. Trump seemed to suggest the counterprotestors were also to blame. He failed to specifically denounce the extremist groups. In fairness, I considered it was possible the president, like others, didn't want to get ahead of the facts about the incident since we didn't know who all of the victims were. I knew deep down, though, that the truth wasn't good. He didn't want to admit it because the violent group was a pro-MAGA crowd.

The bipartisan outcry was immediate. One of the president's staunchest defenders on Capitol Hill,

Senator Orrin Hatch of Utah, joined a number of his colleagues in urging the president to clarify his remarks and condemn the hate groups by name. Meanwhile, white supremacists hailed Trump's statement in their own publications, because they also saw it as a defense of their cause.

On Monday, Attorney General Jeff Sessions labeled the incident an "evil" act of domestic terrorism. White House staff frantically worked to get the president to approve a new statement to make clear he, too, was opposed to white supremacists and neo-Nazis. In the meantime, top CEOs began resigning from administration advisory councils in protest of the president's ambivalence, including the heads of Under Armour, Intel, and Merck. Although he would later inform reporters that his first statement in Charlottesville's violent aftermath was "beautiful," the president yielded and gave a new public statement singling out the hate groups.

On Tuesday, it took a turn for the worse. During a press conference at New York's Trump Tower meant to be about US infrastructure, the president went off on a rant about Charlottesville and seemed to cast aside the revised statements issued the day before. He condemned the vehicular homicide, but then he opined that the "Unite the Right" rally included some "very fine people" and that "the press has treated them absolutely unfairly." The dazed, resigned look on Chief of Staff John Kelly's face went viral; for good reason.

Those of us watching it live had to pick our jaws up off the floor. *What was he talking about?* It was hard for anyone to imagine "very fine people" innocently stumbling across a neo-Nazi rally that was widely publicized in advance. "Very fine people" seemed highly unlikely to join marchers who carried signs with swastikas and bellowed anti-Semitic slogans. David Duke and Richard Spencer, both well-known white supremacists, were not "very fine people."

Trump did not stop there. He defended the alt-right demonstration, comparing the removal of the Confederate leader's statue to bringing down those of the Founding Fathers. "This week, it is Robert E. Lee...I wonder, is it George Washington next? And is it Thomas Jefferson the week after? You know, you have to ask yourself, where does it stop?" He again blamed "both sides" for the violence, including the counterprotestors that he labeled the "alt-left." "Do they have any semblance of guilt?" he asked. This was the real Trump speaking, not the scripted one.

Donald Trump has been accused of being a bigot; whether it is of conviction or convenience is debated. I personally have never believed the president is racist in his heart of hearts. But what difference does it make if the effect is the same? When he makes statements that encourage racists and knows full well he is doing so, it is wrong. More damning than that is his aloofness. The American public can see that the administration is not doing enough to counter racially motivated violence. Why is that? Because ultimately the man at the top doesn't show interest. In the minds of Trump boosters, problems such as white supremacy are an invention of the Left to push an identity-politics agenda. As a result, the president is reluctant to act, hesitant to lead the charge on an issue that might alienate some of his supporters, all the while ignoring a deadly brush-fire sweeping the hearts and minds of a small but menacing faction here at home.

The sense of disappointment throughout the administration was palpable after Charlottesville. We felt the president's reaction revealed an uglier side of his nature: the shallow and demagogic politician, prone to self-inflicted disaster. So many of us were already frustrated by the president's handling of his job. Now, purposefully or not, he was channeling the views of bigots, who were in turn excited that an American leader was sticking up for them. Once people like David Duke are praising you, a normal person quickly figures out they're on the wrong track and corrects course. Not Donald Trump.

Of all the crazy, embarrassing statements we were enduring weekly, his comments about Charlottesville took the cake. It was repugnant. I thought of how the Republican Party, which once helped propel the civil rights movement, now had as its mouthpiece a man whose words fed racial intolerance. I wondered, would he learn anything from this? Could he learn anything from this? And how the hell do I stick around?

I know that's a question many of you are asking: Why didn't anyone leave? God knows it would've been easy. We all have draft resignation letters in our desks or on our laptops. That's the half-teasing, half-true advice you get on day one in the Trump administration or immediately following Senate confirmation: "Be sure to write your resignation letter. You may need it at a moment's notice, or less." Some of us did consider resigning on the spot. One journalist reported a cabinet member saying he would have written a resignation letter, taken it to the president, and "shoved it up his ass." The sentiment was shared. But in the end, no one angrily stormed out. There was no protest resignation.

"Why do people stay?" a close friend asked me at the time. "You all should quit. He's a mess."

"That's why," I responded. *"Because* he's a mess." It was true for a lot of us. We thought we could keep it together. The answer feels more hollow than it used to. Maybe my friend was right. Maybe that was a lost moment, where a rush to the exits would have meant something.

The mood in the administration darkened in the months ahead. The controversy left a permanent bruise on Trump's presidency. We were only partway through our first year, yet I feared—and knew—it was a harbinger of more to come. It was also the moment when I received the answer to that lingering question I had about him. The question was not whether Trump was a model leader. Such a conclusion would have been laughable by that point. The question was whether the presidency would at least instill in this man the ability to be a bigger person than he was, whether he could rise up to meet the moment. That was my hope.

Not long after, as I was walking the State Floor of the White House, I scanned the portraits of American leaders adorning the corridors. One thought started to grip me and never left: Donald Trump does not belong among them. He isn't a man of great character, or good character. He is a man of none.

CHAPTER 3

Fake Views

"We must present to the world not just an America that's militarily strong, but an America that is morally powerful, an America that has a creed, a cause, a vision of a future time when all peoples have the right to self-government and personal freedom. I think American conservatives are uniquely equipped to present to the world this vision of the future—a vision worthy of the American past."
— *Ronald Reagan*

There is a tweet for everything." That's a frequent eye-roll comment from the president's critics. They like to show how Trump takes one position and then, a few years or even days later, tweets out the 180-degree-opposite opinion. It's now a common refrain for people inside his administration, too, who both marvel at and curse the president's uncanny *inability* to stick to his guns.

A cottage industry has cropped up around the phenomenon of his shifting views. One online entrepreneur created a small business out of it. President Flip Flops. The webstore literally sells sandals with a Trump tweet on the left shoe contradicted by a Trump tweet on the right shoe, including gems such as: his claim that the Electoral College was a "disaster for a democracy"; followed by an online post hailing the Electoral College as "actually genius" after he won the election. His tweet citing an "extremely credible source" with rumors about Barack Obama; followed by a warning to his followers: "Remember, don't believe 'sources said'...If they don't name the sources, the sources don't exist." Or his message urging the Obama administration, "DO NOT ATTACK SYRIA" because it would be "VERY FOOLISH"; followed by a tweet praising "our great military" for doing "so well in the Syria attack," which he ordered.

The inconsistencies remind me of something a pollster friend once told me. She explained what she called "the fact-problem test." It was a simple way to determine whether a candidate's "views" were resonating with voters, creating a strong and trusted brand. Ronald Reagan was a high scorer. For instance, you could give a 1980s voter a fake political scenario about any major topic and then ask, "What would Reagan's position be on this matter? X, Y, or Z?" The voter would respond without hesitating. "Z." Reagan communicated his views clearly and acted decisively, so people knew where he stood.

Imagine voters receiving the same fact-problem test for Donald Trump. "What would Trump's position be on this matter? X, Y, or Z?" Fill in whatever scenario you want. Let's say the issue was health care, abortion, trade with China, or guns. I pity the voter who would give a confident answer. Because Trump has flip-flopped on all of them.

He repeatedly called for a "full repeal" of Obamacare as president, and ripped Republicans in Congress for failing to deliver; later, after hanging them out to dry, he said he didn't want a full repeal. He wanted to keep parts of it. He has long said he is "pro-choice," but later while running for president, that he was so deeply "pro-life" that he believed "there has to be some form of punishment" for women who have abortions. Trump said China's government should be labeled a "currency manipulator" and held accountable; then later, "They're not currency manipulators"; and then later, they were "*historic*" (!) currency manipulators. He ranted that "gun control legislation is not the answer!"; then toyed with the idea of supporting it as president; then got lectured by the National Rifle Association and backed away; then tweeted after shootings in Ohio and Texas about "serious discussions" with Congress on gun control legislation; then backed off his pronouncements again. By the time you read this, the president may have flip-flopped on these issues several more times.

The brilliant Abigail Adams, one of our earliest First Ladies and a leader in her own right, once said, "I've always felt that a person's intelligence is directly reflected by the number of conflicting points of view he can entertain simultaneously on the same topic." Donald Trump's problem is he never lands on a final position. His points of view are in constant conflict and liable to change for no reason whatsoever, and certainly not from thoughtful deliberation.

No president in recent history has come into the Oval Office with such a mishmash of ideas and opinions than its current occupant. Ideologically, the Trump White House is like an Etch A Sketch. Every morning the president wakes up, shakes it, and draws something. It might be the same sketch as yesterday. Sometimes it's totally different or impossible to figure out. Nonetheless, he will call a top lieutenant to talk about his drawing, and the entire day will feel like a séance, with officials huddling to divine the mysterious squiggly lines and pretending they represent something meaningful.

Should we care if a president doesn't really stand for anything with consistency? One who is so easily influenced by whomever he happens to speak to last—a cable show host, a member of Congress he likes, his daughter? A president's views on public issues are everything. The opinions he expresses inform the actions of his administration, congressional priorities, and most important of all, public support and trust. How can any of us be comfortable with a president having "fake views," which change by the moment?

This chapter is addressed to Republicans in particular. The GOP purports to be the party of principles, so you should be alarmed that our figurehead's philosophy is not "stick to ideals"—but to throw them at the wall and "see what sticks." If his flip-flopping is any indication, he prioritizes *convenience*, not *conviction*. Add this to the list of absurdities inside the Trump administration, a list that's so long it makes the side effects on prescription drug commercials sound appealing by comparison.

In fairness to the president, there's a lot of bullshit in government. People change direction with the political winds all the time to make sure they're on the "right side" of an issue. They don't want to be out of step with the public, or their base, or their party. That's politics. Sometimes it's actually admirable when a leader considers new information and adjusts preconceived views. That is not Donald Trump. He changes his views without explanation yet somehow convinces diehard Republicans that he possesses a fixed set of beliefs and an ideology, when he does not. He has fooled them into thinking he is a conservative, when he is not. They expect he will be unfailingly loyal to their causes, when he will not.

Trump defenders are bound to disagree. Some have proclaimed him the greatest president since Reagan, while others striving for the preposterous have called him the best since Lincoln. He encourages the comparison. "Wow, highest Poll Numbers in the history of the Republican Party," he tweeted in July 2018. "That includes Honest Abe Lincoln and Ronald Reagan. There must be something wrong, please recheck that poll!" This is the same man who proudly declared on the White House lawn, "I am the Chosen One," gesturing knowingly toward the heavens in front of a gaggle of reporters. He said he was teasing, but he wasn't. Such is the self-perception of Donald J. Trump.

Supporters cite a host of conservative victories under Trump, from judicial appointments to regulatory changes. Admittedly, on those points they have a case. He has advanced a number of conservative goals in ways thought unimaginable before his election. Consider the Supreme Court, which has a stronger conservative bench, or the burdensome red tape that has been slashed on his watch, to the relief of American businesses. Add to it the changes to our insane tax code, which have put more money in Americans' pockets.

Alas, these successes often had little to do with the president's leadership. The credit usually belongs to Republicans in Congress or top aides to the president, who have persuaded him to stick with the program. When he goes wobbly on issues, GOP leaders stage late-night or unplanned interventions, usually by phone.

I remember the morning he woke up and tweeted about the "controversial" vote set to take place in Congress on renewing the National Security Agency's foreign wiretapping authorities. The president railed against the spy powers.

He declared they were used "to so badly surveil and abuse the Trump Campaign." We were blindsided. Up until that moment, the administration had been enthusiastically supporting the bipartisan legislation. The president's flippant remarks threw the future of the bill—and crucial national-security tools—into doubt. Livid Republican leaders phoned the White House to explain the legislation. The president clearly didn't understand, they said. The NSA's spy tools were used to go after bad guys, not to monitor domestic political campaigns. Internally, there was a full-court press to get Trump to walk back his earlier comments. Two hours later, he did, tweeting favorably about the bill: "We need it! Get smart!"

Without these interventions, many times Donald Trump would have wandered into the political wilderness far from the Republican camp. It can take a while to get him to come around, his fear of disappointing "the base" most consistently keeps him in check. In the above case, the president definitely didn't want the GOP to see him as weak on national security, which is why he reversed himself. This should be only a temporary comfort to worried Republicans. Because the base will not matter to Trump if he is reelected in 2020.

The Grand Old Party

Like the rest of the country, members of the Republican Congress didn't take Donald Trump seriously at first. But as he gained steam, they went from agitated to petrified. No one was more concerned than House Speaker Paul Ryan. Ryan once pledged to transform the GOP from a party of "opposition" under eight years of President Obama to a party of "proposition," as he put it, churning out conservative ideas for fixing America. He spent months crafting new policy proposals—from fighting poverty to fixing health care—that he hoped would be embraced by the Republican nominee in 2016. Then Donald Trump showed up.

With the New York businessman on a glide-path to clinching the nomination, the Speaker adjusted course. He was unsure whether the candidate was a real conservative. Would Trump support Republican policies, or sell them all down the river once he was elected? His record showed he was more of a political opportunist than anything. Ryan called a closed-door meeting of his colleagues. They had to box in Donald Trump with their soon-to-be-published GOP agenda. Every elected Republican needed to promote it, he said, which would send a clear message to the candidate: If you win the election, *this* is the party you will be leading and *this* is what it stands for. Don't buck us. As one attendee later retold the story, Ryan looked at his colleagues across the table and said with total assurance: "This is the Trump inoculation plan."

The "Grand Old Party" got its nickname just after the Civil War, an honorific meant to acknowledge its role in saving the Union and ending slavery. The party was founded on the idea that government's role in society should be limited and the freedom of the people should be maximized. The federal bureaucracy had responsibility in certain areas, they believed—trade relationships and national defense among them—but most power should devolve to states and the people themselves.

The GOP's foundations were built on what is known as *classical liberalism*. Before *liberal* was a term associated with Democrats, it meant something very different. Classical liberalism developed over hundreds of years. In a nutshell, it posited that people should be allowed to conduct their lives however they wanted, as long as they didn't violate someone else's liberty. Government existed for the sole purpose of preserving freedom and protecting people from each other. Anything beyond that was government overreach. It became a central belief of classical liberals that individuals are far better positioned to make their own decisions than government is for them; the more control they have over their lives, the more prosperous their societies will be.

Whatever else came to be associated with the GOP, these beliefs were at its core. It is the party's heritage. That was the idea, anyway. Like any group, the Republican Party has evolved. Sometimes it has been more "populist," reacting to the whims of the people and supporting a broader sphere of government action in society, and other times more "libertarian," veering closer to a strict interpretation of its founding principles of limited government.

When Donald Trump came onto the GOP scene, party leaders were concerned about whether he supported, or even understood, the conservative movement. With good reason. Over the last three decades, Trump has changed his political party registration five times. He has been a member of the Independence Party, the Democratic Party, the Republican Party, a registered independent, and then decided he was a Republican again. I doubt during any of these switches that he did much "studying up" on the philosophical identity of each group.

GOP members had a right to be circumspect. In

2004, Trump confessed to CNN, "In many cases, I probably identify more as a Democrat." In 2007, he praised Hillary Clinton and said, "Hillary's always surrounded herself with very good people," adding, "I think Hillary would do a good job [as president]." Incredibly, as a *Republican* presidential candidate in 2015, Trump again repeated that he identified "as a Democrat" on key issues like the economy. In the years up to that point, he donated to the biggest Democrats at all levels of government— Hillary Clinton, Joe Biden, Anthony Weiner, John Kerry, and Harry Reid. He gave money to Andrew Cuomo, Terry McAuliffe, and Eliot Spitzer. It was only after he started to get serious about running for president as a "Republican" that he gave money primarily to Republican candidates.

Trump is not the only president in the modern era to have switched sides. Ronald Reagan famously changed from the Democratic Party to the Republican Party, but the change was driven by principle, and the change stuck. He didn't sway back and forth, again and again. It would be tough for anyone to claim Donald Trump flipped parties on "principle" like Reagan.

Some have sought to dig into Trump's ideological evolution, figuring out what changed or who inspired him to become a Republican. I'll spare them the needless waste of effort. Donald Trump became a conservative when it became politically convenient for him. I have no doubt he would have become the raucous rising star of the Democratic Party, too, if that looked like a shorter path to the Oval Office. Either way, he did with his belief system what he did with any Trump product. He outsourced it for low-cost manufacturing to someone else, then slapped his name on it. A handful of hired minions gave him the bare-bones requirements of a "conservative" platform. And he covered it with gaudy gold plating to make it his own.

This realization—of a wolf in elephant's clothing—dawned on Republican commentators one by one during the 2016 primaries. The most prominent defenders of the conservative faith warned the rest of the GOP that Trump was an apostate. David McIntosh, the head of the conservative Club for Growth, said the candidate was not a "free-market conservative." Rush Limbaugh blasted Trump's support for bloated entitlement programs, engaging in a rhetorical back-and-forth with himself on the air, "Can somebody point to me the conservative on the ballot? What do you mean, Rush? Are you admitting Trump is not a conservative? Damn right I am!" The late columnist Charles Krauthammer wrote, "Trump has no affinity whatsoever for the central thrust of modern conservatism—a return to less and smaller government."

I had my own misgivings like any of them. I watched as Trump spent more time mocking other candidates than he did on substance. The debates became little more than schoolyard brawls when he jumped in. When he did talk about what he stood for, it was often anathema to GOP principles, from his views on socialized medicine to a large federal role in education. I was especially concerned and surprised by Trump's views on the economy, which were far more "interventionist" than the policies the Republican Party had been promoting in recent years.

Donald Trump was not coming off as a conservative, because he wasn't. That's why Republicans tried to erect ideological "roadblocks" to his nomination by pointing out the candidate's sharp deviations from the GOP platform. Those roadblocks did little to stop a man who wasn't driving on the same road. He won primary after primary. Speaker Ryan went forward with his backup option, releasing a platform designed to lock the nominee into accepting Republican orthodoxy. Trump largely ignored that, too, and plowed on toward Election Day victory. The Republicans' "inoculation plan" failed. Indeed, it never stood a chance.

The Wolf in Elephant's Clothing

With the full powers of the Executive Office of the President, Donald Trump has turned the GOP into a mess of contradictions. He confounds party leaders daily with errant statements and conflicting positions. But his actions on the topics nearest and dearest to the GOP—the size of government, national defense, and economic policy—are what is most noteworthy. On balance, the president's handling of those issues has been a net negative for the party and the country.

Big, Beautiful Government

For all President Trump's talk these days about Democrats trying to make America socialist, the reality is that he is the king of big government. The federal bureaucracy is just as large, centralized, careless with spending, and intrusive under Donald Trump as it was when Barack Obama was in office. In many cases, it's bigger. This is an uncomfortable truth for Trump supporters. Rather than hew to traditional conservative beliefs about a limited federal role, Trump has allowed government to balloon. He's especially vexed when we inform him the government will never be large enough or powerful enough to execute his spontaneous propositions.

The US federal budget deficit was actually declining under the Obama administration, from $1.4 trillion in 2009 when Obama took office to $587 billion in 2016, just before he left. Credit for the remarkable downward trend goes to congressional Republicans, who forced a standoff with the White House in 2011. They demanded a budget deal that would bring the deficit under control. The result was the Budget Control Act, a law that slashed federal spending, put strict annual limits on future expenditures, and placed a cap on the government's "credit card." It was considered the conservative "Tea Party" movement's crowning achievement.

Donald Trump was not interested in penny-pinching. He may try to project the image of a man working to save taxpayer dollars, and it's true that he can be talked out of stupid ideas if they cost too much. But that's not because he's trying to save money so it can go back to the American people. He still wants to spend the money, just on things in which *he's* personally interested, such as bombs or border security. Trump recoils at people who are "cheap." Today he is sparing no expense on the management of the executive branch, spending so freely it makes the money-burning days of the Trump Organization look like the five-dollar tables at a Vegas casino. As a result, the budget deficit has increased every single year since Donald Trump took office, returning to dangerous levels. The president is on track to spend a trillion dollars *above* what the government takes in annually.

Just look at 2019. The president proposed a record-breaking $4.7 trillion budget. That's how much he suggested the federal government spend in a single year. Since Trump took office, the US debt—much of which we owe to other countries that we borrow from—has grown by the trillions, to another all-time high of $22 trillion total. To pay off our debts today, according to one estimate, each taxpayer in the United States would need to fork over an average of $400,000. This should set off fiscal tornado sirens across America. We cannot keep borrowing money we can't pay back, otherwise our children will owe a steep and terrible price.

The president also decided to throw the old spending limits out the window. He didn't want to be holding a credit card that would easily max out. So in a deal cut with Nancy Pelosi, he effectively scrapped the conservatives' treasured Budget Control Act and increased spending limits by more than $300 billion annually, adding another

$2 trillion to America's debt over the next decade. It's difficult to capture the significance of this reversal. If President Obama had hatched a similar plan with a GOP House Speaker, Republicans would have been livid.

Conservatives should view this as complete and utter betrayal. Trump promised to do the opposite on federal spending. During the presidential campaign, he said he would eliminate America's debt during his time in office. That's right—*eliminate it.* How he was going to repay trillions in debt during such a short window was never fully explained. But that didn't matter, because it wasn't true. He said it to appease worried conservatives and to assure them that he was "one of them," a budget hawk who wanted to cut spending. More "fake views." Astoundingly, instead of a mutiny against President Trump, GOP congressmen whistled past the graveyard as they went to cast their votes on his disastrous budget deal, proving yet again that Trump has a Darth Vader chokehold on weak-willed Republicans.

Donald Trump has America back on the road to bankruptcy, an area where he has unparalleled expertise for a president of the United States. The small band of fiscal conservatives who remain in the Trump administration warned the president about the eventual dangers of his out-of-control spending addiction. In one such meeting, Trump reportedly said, "Yeah, but I won't be here." I never heard him say those words, but it doesn't come as a surprise. That's how he thinks. What does he care if the federal government goes belly-up? By then it won't be his problem.

Trump also promised on the campaign trail to slash the bloated federal workforce. That, too, appears to have been a head fake. The number of government employees hasn't shrunk much at all under Donald Trump. In fact, as of the second half of 2019, the federal workforce was on the rise again, to its largest levels since the end of the Obama administration. The president hasn't made the issue a priority in his engagement with Congress, despite countless opportunities to bring it up in budget negotiations.

Trump has worked hard in the meantime to make the executive branch even more active, not less. While he's cut regulations, he's also issued a flurry of executive orders to bypass Congress and its elected representatives. Trump attacked Obama for doing the same, calling it "a basic disaster" and undemocratic. "We have a president that can't get anything done so he just keeps signing executive orders all over the place," he said. "Why is Barack Obama constantly issuing executive orders that are major power grabs of authority?" That was before Trump himself took office. Now he issues orders at a rate rivaling his Democratic predecessors. In his first three years, Bill Clinton issued 90 executive orders. In that same time period, Barack Obama issued 110. Donald Trump issued 120 before his third year was over.

The Trump administration is not a rewarding place for a fiscal conservative to work. Our attempts to get the president to care have mostly failed. Saving money is usually boring to him. When he gets interested in ending what he determines are wasteful programs—which for him are very specific initiatives like environmental projects he's been told about or dollars sent to a country he's angry with—he doesn't understand why the initiatives cannot be stopped with a finger snap. People remind him again that it requires consistent attention and time. He has to work with Congress. But that's too much effort. A few of us held out hope that as another election rolled around he'd get more interested in reducing spending and runaway agency budgets in order to satisfy conservatives. Instead he made a quick deal with Speaker Pelosi because it was easier and it gave him more cash. The callous trade was a tombstone placed atop our budget-balancing daydreams.

For a man who loves "big" things, Trump

wanted his government the same way. This should not be a surprise.

Indefensible Defense

On defense and homeland security, the story appears better on the surface. The president has increased military spending (albeit at the cost of heaping piles of debt). He has focused on modernizing US forces and raising pay for our troops. And he has made securing the country and the border one of the highest priorities of his presidency.

In reality, Trump has been a disaster for the Pentagon. He refers to leaders of the military not as nonpartisan defenders of the republic, but as "his generals," whom he can move around as he pleases, like knights on a chess board. It's tough to listen to him talk like this. Some of these leaders have lost children in the defense of the nation. They have answered the knock at the door from men and women standing there to tell them the most heart-wrenching news a parent can hear, that their child is gone forever. Yet they are on the receiving end of orders barked by a man who cowered at the thought of military service. The patriots who are still in uniform will not come out and say it because they don't want to openly disagree with their commander in chief, but many are appalled by Trump's lack of decorum and his imprudent leadership of the armed forces.

Time and again, he has put our armed forces in a terrible position by trying to pull the military into political debates or using it to demonstrate his own toughness. This began before he entered office. As a candidate, Trump suggested the military and intelligence agencies embrace torture as a tactic against America's enemies, vowing, "I would bring back waterboarding. And I would bring back a hell of a lot worse than waterboarding." Analysts pointed out that such statements are used by terrorists for propaganda, helping them recruit supporters by touting America's supposed cruelty. It feeds their narrative, putting US forces in danger overseas. Fortunately, the president was persuaded to drop the subject early in his term by the incoming team, who realized Trump's flip-flopping would impact national defense most of all.

The damage the president has done to our security is a consequence of his terrible foreign policy choices, an area where Trump's instincts are so backward that we will devote an entire chapter to addressing them. For now, take Iran as an example. President Trump took office eager to meet face-to-face with Iran's leaders, who run one of the most anti-American governments in the world. "Anytime they want," he said. No preconditions. This is something a US president has never done, for good reason. Iran's government has the blood of American soldiers on its hands. They are responsible for the deaths of hundreds of US troops in Iraq and Afghanistan. Giving them an audience with the leader of the free world would put them on equal footing and be priceless media fodder for their use back home. It would also demonstrate to Iranian dissidents that America was embracing the brutal regime, not opposing it. Donald Trump didn't understand or care about any of that, and military leaders' stomachs churned at the president's offer.

Then Trump's views began to change. He witnessed Iran's hostile behavior and recognized appeasement wasn't the best course of action. His internal pendulum swung hard in the other direction. After Iran shot down an American surveillance drone in June 2019, the president wanted a super-muscular response. Pentagon officials warned against escalation with Tehran, but Trump reportedly called for a military strike anyway. When warplanes were in the air ten minutes out from the target, he apparently decided to call it off, caving to the advice of skeptics including Fox News host Tucker Carlson. Only a few weeks later, the pendulum swung again. He was back to suggesting to aides that he might sit down with Iran's leaders in a face-to-face meeting, which many of us believed would be a colossal mistake. Trump teased the possibility of a G7 meeting in France.

When Trump's flip-flopping is about something like new army uniforms ("very expensive," he once lamented, but on the other hand, "beautiful"), it is exhausting. When it's about air strikes, it's terrifying. The president's impetuousness poses a danger to our military, the full extent of which will not be known for years. He is more than a minor headache for the Pentagon. He is a blinding migraine. Those who have served at the highest levels of the Pentagon, who have sat with Trump in moments of decision, know all too well. On a weekly basis, they shield men and women in uniform from the knowledge, as best they can, of just how undisciplined the commander in chief is above them and how he treats the US military like it's part of a big game of Battleship. Our warriors risk everything to venture into the darkest corners of the world to hunt those who would do us harm. They deserve better for their inviolable code of duty than a man lacking a basic moral compass.

It's scary how we, his appointees, have become accustomed to this. I once walked out of a meeting with the president, and a visibly shaken briefer, who was new to the Trump circus, pulled me aside.

"Are you kidding me?" he remarked. Moments earlier Trump expressed a spur-of-the-moment reversal about a military mission. He wanted to go another direction, and his change of heart was followed by a presidential order to act, straightaway.

"What should we do?" the briefer asked nervously. "He wants us to scrap everything the agency was planning."

"Relax," I assured him. "We aren't going to do anything. I swear he'll change his mind tomorrow."

I was wrong. The president changed his mind later that afternoon.

Then there is homeland security. For conservatives, this is a subset of "defense" and the government's overall obligation to protect its citizens. For President Trump, it is a centerpiece of his agenda. He ran on the promise to bring the border under control and to support agents on the frontlines. Of all the random issues he brings up unprompted in meetings and events, the award for biggest Trump non sequitur goes to "The Wall."

It's a running joke in the White House that one of the worst jobs in the administration belongs to the poor souls charged with designing the president's border wall. Trump, of course, talks about the wall all the time with a gleam in his eye. Running for president, he vowed that he would build "a great wall, and nobody builds walls better than me, believe me, and I'll build them very inexpensively… And I will have Mexico pay for that wall. Mark my words." He admonished rival candidate Jeb Bush for talking about border fencing: "It's not a fence, Jeb. It's a WALL, and there's a BIG difference."

I have to admit, it's knee-slappingly hilarious to watch Trump tackle this issue. In late 2015, he said his wall would "be made of hardened concrete…rebar and steel." At one point in 2017, he proposed that the wall be solar powered to generate clean electricity. A month later, he said that "you have to be able to see through it." The wall was no longer a concrete slab, but "a steel wall with openings." Then the wall became "artistically designed steel slats." Then, in 2018, the president claimed he could have "a steel wall—or it could be a steel fence—but it will be more powerful than any of the concrete walls that we're talking about." At the end of 2018 he said "an all concrete Wall was NEVER ABANDONED, as has been reported by the media," only to tweet less than a week later that "We are now planning a Steel Barrier rather than concrete." Midway through 2019, he flipped again, touting the "brand-new" "high steel *and* concrete Wall" that he'd already built and previewed that there was much more to come.

Officials would come out of meetings on the subject looking like they'd stepped off the Gravitron at the county fair. The president was constantly changing the design. Ten feet high or fifty feet high? Electric fence or not electric fence? He couldn't make up his mind, officials complained. They were pulling their hair out in frustration. Trump's shifting preference in aesthetics seemed to be matched only by his shifting explanations for the construction timeline. At various times, Trump told us construction was under way, then he said Democrats were stopping the wall from being built altogether, then that Congress needed to act, then that his critics were wrong and so much wall was being built, then that the courts were standing in the way, and then—never mind all of that about Congress and the courts—he could build it alone and "we'll have the whole [border] sealed up" by the end of 2020.

Here's the truth. Trump has barely built any wall, and his policies have been a thorough failure when it comes to border security. By all accounts, most of what the president has built is replacement of old fences at the border. If there are really hundreds of miles of new wall on the way, as he nervously promises voters, experts say it still won't solve the problem. Even with a giant concrete wall (or steel fence, or concrete-steel wall-fence) across the entire border, migrants can still come to our border and file for protected status. Then they are let into the United States for years while their cases are reviewed. *That* is what Republicans begged Trump to address, but instead of using his political capital to fix the broken laws, he fixated on one of his favorite pastimes—a construction project. The result is that the system will remain broken well past his presidency.

In the process of bungling border security, Donald Trump has obliterated America's reputation as a nation of immigrants. This is a deeply Republican, conservative, classical liberal conception—that the United States is a refuge for those seeking a better life. Such was the condition of the republic at the moment of its founding and ever since. The United States was molded by people who left home in faraway places, by idealistic risk takers and hard workers who fought the odds to reach a literal new world. Our republic was not rooted in "blood and soil." It was rooted in a shared aspiration for a fresh start. However, not being a man of history, Trump never adopted this view.

A shocked aide walked out of a ⸢
the Oval Office one day, came to my o⸢⸢
recounted an anecdote about a conversation w⸢⸢
the president. They'd been meeting on another
topic, when Trump off-roaded onto a tangent
about immigration, complaining about the number of people crossing the border.

"We get these women coming in with like seven
children," he told his listeners, briefly attempting
a Hispanic accent. "They are saying, 'Oh, please
help! My husband left me!' They are useless. They
don't do anything for our country. At least if they
came in with a husband we could put him in the
fields to pick corn or something."

The handful of attendees in the room shifted
uncomfortably in their chairs but said nothing, the aide reported. They didn't even know
what to say. This is how the president of the
United States thinks and speaks about people
who would give their lives (and sometimes do)
to reach America. Whenever these quotes find
their way to the press, a mid-level communications staffer is dispatched to say Trump was joking. I assure you he isn't.

No matter what his supporters will tell you,
no matter what some appointees will try to convince you of, Donald Trump is anti-immigrant.

He might be in a meeting about missile defense, but inside he is probably thinking about his wall... about shutting down immigration to the United States...about *the Mexicans*. Of the latter, he said, "They're not sending their best...They're bringing drugs. They're bringing crime. They're rapists. And some, I assume, are good people." Imagine how that makes an entire population of Mexican-Americans feel. Sadly, you hear little repudiation of Trump's anti-immigrant rhetoric from his homeland security officials, who appear to be living in a dazed state of Stockholm syndrome.

The president has also weighed the idea of dropping the number of foreign refugees admitted into the United States—which tend to be people fleeing persecution from poor, non-white countries—down to zero. Yes, you read that correctly: zero... zilch...nada. He already slashed the number to historic lows. In the meantime, he's announced a host of tight restrictions on potential new immigrations, including the imposition of a wealth test. I wonder if, in all his years in New York, Trump ever saw the words at the base of the Statue of Liberty, which read in part: "Give me your tired, your poor, Your huddled masses yearning to breathe free." If he did, it didn't mean anything to him.

The bottom line for Republicans is this: The

United States can have an open door without having "open borders," but we cannot preserve the country we love by slamming that door in the faces of those who most aspire to join our nation.

Trading Away Principles

The president's biggest abdication of conservative policies is in the realm of economics. Republicans have long stood for free trade, believing the open exchange of goods is a fundamental right. The United States is more prosperous than any nation in history because of it. However, Donald Trump is a dogged protectionist. He has created new barriers to trade, justified by an inverted view of economics that has been discredited for hundreds of years.

Fundamentally, Trump does not understand how trade works. When experts try to explain it to him, he either half listens or only hears what he wants to hear. What he wants to hear, of course, is that his trade wars with other countries are a brilliant move and a big success. His favorite weapon in these economic conflicts is the tariff. The president believes adding fees to incoming foreign goods "will bring in FAR MORE wealth to our Country." We've endured years of him spewing this false notion.

Many experts know this is crazy. Why would a president deny Americans the opportunity to pay less for their products? Why would he purposefully make the goods they buy more expensive? As one economist explained, it should be in the public interest "in every country" to let the people "buy whatever they want from those who sell it cheapest...The proposition is so very manifest that it seems ridiculous to take any pains to prove it." This wasn't a recent observation. It was the father of capitalism, Adam Smith, writing in the 1700s. His point is more relevant than ever.

To understand how far off the reservation the president has gone, you have to look at the world through his soda straw. Trump believes placing a tariff—or tax—on incoming goods will make us rich. Let's say he imposed a 20 percent tariff on sweaters from India. In Trump's mind, that means for every thirty-dollar sweater shipped from India, we will collect six dollars in fees, meaning the Indians basically would be *paying us* to buy their sweaters. Sounds good, right? It gets better. With the resulting higher price of sweaters, US companies can afford to get back into the sweater business, and they start competing with India because the fee only applies to foreign products. So they can sell them at a slightly lower cost to Americans.

The result is new jobs in the US sweater industry. Win-win for America!

Not so fast. This infantile logic has been repeated for ages, despite Adam Smith's timeless words. Here is what really happens. As soon as the tariff is placed on sweaters, the extra cost will be passed to consumers. The Indians won't pay the six dollars, *Americans will pay for it.* Those same Americans will be forced to spend more money on clothing than they were before. Multiply that across the country and that's *billions and billions of dollars* extra they will have to spend on sweaters, and less on other products they need. Sure, some US companies will be incentivized to start making sweaters, creating low-paying jobs. But what will go unnoticed is the impact everywhere else— the *billions of dollars* other companies will *lose* because Americans are spending it on something they shouldn't be. Better-paying jobs will disappear elsewhere.

The economics are painfully obvious. Tariffs don't work. They are just a massive tax on Americans, robbing them of their hard-earned money. Regrettably, no living human has been able to help the president see this reality. Believe me, many among us have tried. His convoluted view of economics is beyond repair.

The debate has created schisms within the team. Treasury Secretary Steven Mnuchin has fought behind closed doors for a level-headed approach to tariffs. He has recommended against some of the arbitrary and sudden moves made by the president. Mnuchin has also repeatedly attempted to ease panic in private industry by downplaying the trade wars, only to be rebuked by advisors at the White House for supposedly speaking out of turn. Folks such as Peter Navarro have seen their stock with Trump rise for cheerleading his actions, although they still privately admit frustration because there's no telling whether he'll change his mind at any given moment and raise fees further without a plan. As with any other issue, the reasonable voices are being sidelined.

Conservatives must admit this is "back-door" big government. Trump helped push a major tax-cut bill through Congress in 2017, but the consequences of his tariffs will cost the American people more than the money they saved from the legislation, according to estimates. This is a sneaky and contemptible way for the president to raise taxes without people realizing it. Trump knows this is the case. He's already talked with aides about how he'll spend the extra money from his tariff taxes. In a news conference, he also threw around the possibility that some of it might be spent on disaster response. Tomorrow, it might be an addition to the White House or extra border wall, who knows.

I am not making the argument that there are no circumstances which warrant limitations on, or the cessation of, trade with foreign countries. Throughout our history, there have been points in which we've decided it's not in America's interest to trade with certain nations, particularly when we are engaged in armed conflict against an aggressor. I've argued to fellow Trump administrational officials that governments such as China do not deserve to have access to certain US goods, which could allow them to spy on their people or gain a competitive military edge. But we must also recognize that free trade is one of our most potent weapons to lift people out of poverty and empower them to take control over their destinies, rather than allowing autocrats to dictate their future.

The larger concern here at home is that, as he ratchets up his trade wars, the president could trigger a recession and wreck the economy. Deep inside he must share this concern. It's probably one of the reasons he lashes out at agency heads and advisors who have warned him about the consequences of high tariffs. In the meantime, Trump is acting like a dictator. At one point, he tweeted, "Our great

American companies are hereby ordered to immediately start looking for an alternative to China." That's not how a democratic system works, Mr. President. You can't "order" American companies where to make their products. The markets have been spooked by his increasingly unhinged behavior on the matter, and top CEOs have warned the president he needs to reverse course.

It might be too late. Trump's anti-trade actions are hurting Americans at this very moment. Estimates show the economy has already lost hundreds of thousands of jobs because of his trade war. If Trump continues down this path, the prices on everything from phones to furniture will go up further. Every industry will ultimately be impacted by the ripple effects. Farmers, manufacturers, you name it. Other countries are retaliating already with their own tariffs, which magnifies the problem. Working-class and poor Americans will be hit hardest. They are the ones who rely on low prices to run households where there is little margin for financial error. If Trump continues to live in an economic Twilight Zone, these people will be forced to work longer hours and extra jobs just to make ends meet.

Trade should not be used as a weapon of war in times of peace. It's a war that everyone loses. It's time for the GOP to see the light. The president's economic policies are bad for Americans, contrary to conservative principles, and cruel—not unlike their architect.

Party's Over

After Mitt Romney's failure to unseat President Obama in 2012, the Republican Party had a come-to-Jesus moment. How could we have lost the election? It seemed so obvious to the GOP leadership that Barack Obama was out of touch with mainstream America. In their eyes, the election should have been a cakewalk. But Romney got walloped 332–206 in the Electoral College. It was clear that the Republicans were the ones who were out of touch. Those who know Mitt believed he would have been a capable leader, but he was unable to connect with the broader swath of the electorate that he needed.

The Republican National Committee (RNC) commissioned an election "autopsy report." The results were stark. Released four months after voting day, the hundred-page document highlighted the party's problems with minorities, women, and young people. It said conservative policies had strong foundations but needed to be recast for new audiences. Republicans should bring more people under the tent, the authors wrote, but instead they were ostracizing them.

"Young voters are increasingly rolling their eyes at what the Party represents, and many minorities wrongly think that Republicans do not like them or want them in the country," the document declared. "If Hispanic Americans hear that the GOP doesn't want them in the United States, they won't pay attention to our next sentence." The report urged Republicans to focus on "broadening the base of the Party," especially being more inclusive of "Hispanic, black, Asian, and gay Americans"—and especially female voters, whom the party was failing to recruit. The findings were released at a press conference by RNC chairman Reince Priebus. Three years later, Reince, of course, would become Trump's first White House chief of staff.

If you've been at least half-conscious during the Trump presidency, you probably know the president has followed virtually none of this advice. In fact, it seems as if he's *deliberately* written a counter-playbook, flagrantly dismissing the RNC's recommendations and alienating the populations the GOP needs to reach. On Donald Trump's watch, the party has become less fiscally conservative, more divisive, less diverse, more anti-immigrant, and less relevant. In the meantime, he has saddled the Republican brand with uniquely noxious baggage, leaving others to manage a "big-tent" party that will eventually have few people left under its canopy.

How did this happen, you ask? Well, if there's a theme to Trump's life—in politics, business, or family—it's that he's disloyal. Republicans gave the keys to the kingdom to a man who paid hush money to shut up a porn star he'd been sleeping with while married to his third wife, who'd recently given birth to their son. Are we surprised he's run afoul of the party's most cherished ideals? If elected to a second term, he will cheat on naive Republicans over and over again. When asked about whether he might end the disastrous tariffs to which he has wedded himself, the president unintentionally summed up his entire political philosophy: "Yeah, sure. Why not?…Might as well. I have second thoughts about everything." Could it get more ironic than that? It did, when Trump backtracked on the comment itself.

Conservatives dreaming that Donald Trump is our savior need to wake up. Not only is he *not* a conservative, he represents a long-term threat to the Republican Party and what it purports to stand for. He is redefining us to a degree that makes our platform incoherent. Those cheering him on to a second term—with foaming-at-the-mouth excitement that he is "totally owning" the Left—are unknowingly nailing coffins into the GOP, cementing an end to the party as we know it and taking us into inhospitable territory.

Let me put a finer point on it. If Republicans believe the president's handling of their core issues is acceptable, then there is nothing left of the party but its name. Yes, there are still lone-ranger conservatives trying to advance traditional GOP causes from inside the administration, but Trump's leadership of the party (or lack thereof) will be what's remembered, not the cleanup job of his lieutenants.

The president's betrayal of the conservative faith may not be problematic for some reading this book. You might be comfortable with larger bureaucracies, debt spending, or protectionist economics. That's your prerogative. But the president has transformed the long arm of government into a wrecking ball to go after something else *much* more fundamental than the GOP agenda. Every American, regardless of political affiliation, should pay attention.

CHAPTER 4

Assault on Democracy

"Power always thinks it has a great soul and vast views beyond the comprehension of the weak, and that it is doing God's service when it is violating all His laws."
— John Quincy Adams

It didn't take long for President Trump to start turning the powers of his office against the foundations of our democracy. The White House culture was primed for abuses of executive authority from the start, given that Trump spent most of his pre-government life in positions where he had almost total control. These organizations didn't require a collaborative, democratic approach to governance. He didn't have to build bipartisan coalitions or respect a sprawling bureaucracy. It was his show, and it was all about his victories, his ratings, and his name atop big buildings. Following the 2016 election, in which he expressed the custom-

165

ary words of political unity and solidarity, Donald Trump quickly pivoted, eyeing ways to use *his* White House and taxpayer-funded federal investigators—whom he thinks of as *his* investigators— to go after political enemies.

Most Americans shrug at Trump's bombast. Surely he doesn't really want to investigate and jail Democrats who opposed him. This is just another feature of his outlandish entertainment persona. He can't put Hillary Clinton behind bars because he doesn't like her. Right? Donald Trump thinks he can. He is serious about his commands to prosecute and persecute anyone who challenges him. Many of us have come to learn the hard way how angry he gets when the law and *his* lawyers in the administration do not bend to presidential dictates.

Trump's anger reaches its apex when his unethical bidding is not carried out. Advisors might be sitting around the Oval Office, ostensibly to discuss monetary policy or some other issue, and we will suddenly see the president's eyes darken. He'll glance around the room, fidget with the Diet Coke in front of him, and then launch into a long harangue about how his lawyers have failed him, how the attorney general has failed him, how this person or that person needs to be investigated. One time, apropos of nothing, he launched into a tirade about Attorney General Jeff Sessions, who by then was long gone: "Man, he is one of the *stupidest* creatures on this earth God ever created!" The aides in the room tried not to look at one another. Hoping the storm would pass, they wondered as usual, "What does this have anything to do with… anything?"

Trump is particularly frustrated that the Justice Department hasn't done more to harass the Clintons. In his first year in office, he complained to Jeff Sessions that the department hadn't investigated people who deserved it, citing the Hillary Clinton email scandal. Days later he tweeted about the issue, writing, "Where is the Justice Dept?" and noted that there was "ANGER & UNITY" over a "lack of investigation" into the former secretary of state. "DO SOMETHING!" he demanded. The directive was not given to anyone in particular, but it's obvious to whom Trump was speaking. However, Sessions was effectively recused from the matter since it was tied to the Russia investigation.

In December 2017, the president pulled Jeff aside after a cabinet meeting for what was intended to be a private conversation. "I don't know if you could un-recuse yourself," Trump told him, according to the notes of an aide, who believed the president was talking about investigating Hillary Clinton.

"You'd be a hero. Not telling you to do anything." The president reportedly mused that he could order General Sessions to investigate if he wanted to, but then added that he wasn't going to do that. We were all familiar with these "wink, nods" from Trump. He suggests he *can* order someone to do something, but he hopes he doesn't have to do it explicitly—that way he's not tied to the outcome. Trump's little hints are in fact improper demands masquerading as innocent suggestions, and the administration's history is strewn with them. In any event Jeff didn't budge, surely a contributing factor to his eventual firing.

Trump nominated another attorney general, and right away he started telegraphing similar requests. In a March 2019 interview, the president sent not-so-subtle signals to recently confirmed attorney general Bill Barr, telling a reporter that he hoped Barr would "do what's fair" when it came to investigating Clinton. Not long after, he again took to Twitter, openly calling for an investigation into the "crimes committed" by his 2016 Democratic opponent. The messages weren't meant for non-profit groups or part-time investigators to take up the cause. They were clearly meant for the Justice Department. He was skirting the lines of propriety once again. Presidents are not supposed to influence investigative decisions like this, but Trump knew what he was doing. Bill Barr certainly knew. All of us knew.

Our Founders had many differences, but most were united in their apprehension of powerful presidents. They had just broken free of a tyrannical king, after all. Revolutionary-era thinkers discussed the topic ad nauseam. As American historian Bernard Bailyn explained, the Founders' conversations on power "centered on its essential characteristic of aggressiveness: its endlessly propulsive tendency to expand itself beyond legitimate boundaries. Like water, it will flow into whatever space it can reach and fill it."

Thus, the American colonists concluded that protecting liberty required putting checks on the wielders of authority. They built institutions meant to be circuit breakers on government power. Under a system of checks and balances, they hoped even the worst intentions of public officials would be frustrated by the machinery itself. This was the rationale for divvying up responsibility by creating an executive branch, run by a president; counterbalancing it with a legislative branch, consisting of the House and the Senate; and further leveling the playing field with a judicial branch, which contained the courts and the US Supreme Court as the ultimate arbiter of the law of the land.

The Trump presidency is one of the biggest challenges to our nation's checks-and-balances system in modern times. Donald Trump has abused his power to undermine all three branches of government, at times flagrantly and at times in secret. In the process, he has weakened institutions vital to the functioning of our democracy, assailing them as "corrupt." Trump is not fazed by the precedent that he is setting by making it easier for his successors to wield the executive office for personal or political gain. In fact, he is actively working to break free of the protections inherent in the American system meant to limit that power.

We ought to care about that. A lot.

Burying the Deep State

Theodore Roosevelt was no one's idea of the Republican "establishment." Many traditional Republicans despised him. Throughout his career, he was considered a renegade, a maverick, a guy who liked to shake up the system. Once he succeeded to the presidency, he also understood that he couldn't change government on his own. In his autobiography, Roosevelt offered a reflection on those who helped him, including his cabinet and the large group of people within the federal bureaucracy.

"As for the men under me in executive office, I could not overstate the debt of gratitude I owe them," Roosevelt wrote. "From the heads of the departments, the Cabinet officers, down, the most striking feature of the administration was the devoted, zealous, and efficient work that was done as soon as it became understood that the one bond of interest among all of us was the desire to make the Government the most effective instrument in advancing the interests of the people[.]"

More dissonant words could not be spoken about the Trump administration. Rather than affectionately praise the civil service, the current president has launched a brutal assault on them. We are talking about the millions of people who carry out the daily duties of government, whether it is delivering the mail or monitoring economic developments. They act as a "check" on power by making sure the laws are executed faithfully and not subverted by a rogue politician. These days, however, such people are routinely mocked, maligned, ignored, and undercut by the Executive Office of the President. To Trump, their ranks are replete with traitors, an evil "Deep State" out to get him and destroy his presidency.

Early on, he claimed he didn't like that phrase. In an interview with the *Hill* newspaper, Trump said he avoided it because "it sounds so conspiratorial." He added, "And believe it or not I'm really not a conspiratorial person." This was like the Marlboro man saying he wasn't a smoker. It wasn't remotely believable. As the *Hill* pointed out, Trump used the phrase only two weeks earlier to describe an opinion piece written by...me. The Deep State was a threat to democracy, he claimed in a tweet, but what he really meant was that it was a threat to *him* because he was being exposed for who he really was.

Those seeking Trump's favor, or money from his supporters, have made repeated references to the term. They've written variations of the same book—from Jason Chaffetz's *The Deep State: How an Army of Elected Bureaucrats Protected Barack Obama and Is Working to Destroy the Trump Agenda*, to Jerome Corsi's *Killing the Deep State: The Fight to Save President Trump*, to George Papadopoulos's *Deep State Target: How I Got Caught in the Crosshairs of the Plot to Bring Down President Trump*, to

Corey Lewandowski and David Bossie's *Trump's Enemies: How the Deep State is Undermining His Presidency*, and a collection of alliterative titles by Judge Jeanine Pirro, also making the exact same points: Deep inside the government are a group of people out to destroy democracy, Donald Trump, and America.

Since one of those people, according to the president, is me, I would like to take the opportunity to clear the air and respond with a better-substantiated allegation: Trump is out of his mind. I've worked closely with civil servants for many years, whether inside or outside of government. Generally they are good, patriotic Americans who want to serve their country. While some have strong political views like any citizen, the vast majority don't let it affect their work, and regardless of who is leading the White House, they do their jobs. They don't conspire to secretly reverse the policies of the administration in power.

Do you think your mail carrier is having secret meetings to destroy Donald Trump? Do you think federal law enforcement agents, whose culture leans conservative, sit around trying to find ways to get Democrats elected? Is the Pentagon's librarian a mole for Bernie Sanders? The president's claim of a Deep State sounds preposterous because it is. The person intent on destroying democratic foundations is Donald Trump, not the honorable public servants who go to work every day to make sure our government runs—to get Social Security checks out on time, to protect communities from criminals, to keep food and prescription drugs safe from contamination, to uphold our Constitution.

Don't believe it? Consider this: The administration can't even consistently define who exactly is part of the "Deep State," and it changes depending on the day. Who exactly is part of "the Deep State" in Trump's world depends on the day. The term is used to dismiss any agency, report, finding, anonymous quote, news story, or other mode of disagreement with the president. Someone in the government differs with President Trump on global warming? That's the Deep State. A report comes out that says Trump officials have violated ethics laws? That's someone from the Deep State. Lawyers tell the president he can't do something? The Deep Staters are at it again!

Sean Hannity once devoted part of his cable news program to what he called "The Mueller Crime Family," including supposedly nefarious individuals who were part of the Deep-State plot to investigate Donald Trump. One of them was his own deputy attorney general, Rod Rosenstein.

Rosenstein has since won praise from President Trump for his public service, even though the president once retweeted a meme showing Rod behind bars for treason. Which means that members of the "Deep State" really are just people whom Trump doesn't like. Once he likes them, they aren't in it anymore.

The concept has fueled a paranoid and secretive atmosphere across our administration. The White House constantly shuts out and shuts up the public servants of the executive branch, often with the president's blessing, because of suspicion they are disloyal. Meetings are often held for "politicals only," a term used to describe settings where only presidential appointees are welcomed. Sometimes such meetings are held inside the secure White House Situation Room when they have nothing to do with classified information because aides don't want to risk the possibility that a non-political employee might overhear the development of a controversial policy.

The president is alert to this as well, as he is wary when he sees faces he doesn't recognize. If ever experts from within the administration's bureaucracy are brought into sensitive White House discussions, they must be the "trusted" ones. Skepticism about career staff is so intense that sometimes Trump aides deliberately disclose false information in meetings to see if it ends up in the press so they can root out suspected traitors. (The people who do this are the ones you'd expect, and I've seen them hypocritically leak to the press to promote themselves, despite running their own anti-leak operations.) What this means is that Trump is limiting information he hears from within his own government to more inexperienced political types who tend to agree with him in the first place and who he perceives are personally loyal.

The worst part is that America's public servants, whose jobs we are paying for with our tax dollars, are not trusted to do their jobs. We have a government filled with experts on every topic imaginable, from award-winning medical professionals to world-class economists. They're not useful if they're ignored, yet the White House has given implicit sanction to departments and agencies to relocate or otherwise dismiss these voices when they cause problems for the administration's agenda. At a bare minimum, the work of such government employees is frequently left on the cutting room floor.

A common silencing tactic is to tell an office it's "under policy review." That means politicals are trying to decide if the office will be elevated, moved, disbanded, or otherwise reorganized. With their futures hanging in the balance, those employees try not to cause problems while they are stuck in a holding pattern. As a result, many having been standing down on their work for the entirety of the administration, such as scientists focused on climate change or health experts wary of environmental deregulation. If some Trump politicals are hoping these functions will wither in the meantime or people will leave in frustration, they are getting their wish. We are losing talented professionals every single day because of the president.

The result is that our sprawling government is often run by a skeleton crew of partisans. Important issues get neglected with regularity. In fact, a good chunk of the crises we deal with at the highest levels of government emerge, in part, because no one has an eye on the ball. Some of the stupidest actions you've seen our administration take were the result of a plan hatched by a group so tiny that it couldn't see the mountain of secondary consequences right in front of them. Good advice is getting ignored because it isn't being sought in the first place. Even the policies the president *wants* to champion—such as education reform—are getting dropped because there are not enough trusted people around him to pay attention (a reality that led Education secretary Betsy DeVos to admit that "education clearly has not been at the top of [the president's] list of priorities"). Ultimately, with the civil service boxed out of running our government, the American people are getting less than what they pay for, and much less than what they deserve.

The most illustrative example of Trump-maligned government employees is the US intelligence community. These agencies, such as the Central Intelligence Agency and National Security Agency, have some of the most important jobs in America. I wish more Americans could meet these patriots in person to fully grasp their devotion to duty and country. On a day-to-day basis, they are responsible for keeping us safe, going to work in places they cannot discuss to solve problems they must not reveal. Their most stinging defeats are put on public display, while their greatest victories in protecting the American people are celebrated in silence. Many risk their lives—and some give them—without their hard work ever being known. Think about that. It's one thing to lose your life, but to willingly give up your legacy on top of it is an act of eternal sacrifice. This is the ethos that defines the intelligence community.

Donald Trump's attacks on America's covert workforce began before he was elected. He resented the intelligence community's conclusions that the

Russians were interfering in the 2016 election to his benefit. Advisors urged Trump during the campaign to call out the Russians publicly and to disavow their meddling. He had to take a stand, they said, but Trump was unmoved. During one debate-prep session, a member of the team spoke up. He said the candidate needed to acknowledge the intelligence and use the debate stage as a platform to denounce Moscow. If he was going to show solidarity with Secretary Clinton on anything, this was it.

"Yeah, I don't buy it," he said dismissively, waving his hand. "It's total bullshit."

He was egged on by Mike Flynn, an intelligence community dropout who eventually became Trump's first national security advisor but was soon removed for lying about his contacts with Russia. "He's right," Flynn later agreed. "It's all politicized bullshit."

People around him were stunned. What did he say? Why on earth did they think the intelligence had been made up?

As the former head of the Defense Intelligence Agency (DIA), Flynn knew better. As the Republican nominee, Trump should have as well; he'd already started getting official US intelligence briefings. The bizarre reaction stoked fears, including within Trump's circle, that he was somehow in

Putin's pocket. Once elected, he went on to further deride the official assessments, telling reporters who asked about the spy agencies' conclusions aboard Air Force One, "I mean, give me a break. They're political hacks." That's one way to describe people who would give their lives for the country. His casual dismissal of assessments by intelligence experts was disturbing. The intelligence community had been working hard since its major error about weapons of mass destruction in Iraq to strengthen information gathering and analysis. Without their dedication, we never would have found Osama bin Laden or thwarted deadly attacks against the United States, yet Trump is willing to put his "gut" instincts ahead of their expertise.

Donald Trump wasn't always so dismissive of the intel community. At points he tried to stand up for them. Trump repeatedly faulted Barack Obama for allegedly skipping intelligence briefings. During the 2016 campaign, he seemed to imply the professionals sent to brief him (whom he said he had "great respect for") felt alienated by Obama, who supposedly didn't take their advice. "In almost every instance, and I could tell—I'm pretty good with body language—I could tell they were not happy. Our leaders did not follow what they were recommending." That all changed when he decided they were out to get him as part of some Obama conspiracy. Once elected, Trump suggested a president doesn't need daily intelligence briefings. "I get it when I need it," he told Fox News's Chris Wallace. "I'm, like, a smart person. I don't have to be told the same thing in the same words every single day for the next eight years."

When he does sit down for a briefing on sensitive information, it's the same as any other Trump briefing. He hears what he wants to hear, and disregards what he doesn't. Intelligence information must comport to his worldview for it to stick. If it doesn't, it's "not very good." As a result, the president of the United States is often ignorant on the most serious national security threats we face and is, therefore, ill-prepared to defend against them. In fact, I'd submit that he's less informed than he should be on almost every major global threat, from nuclear weapons proliferation to cyber security.

Trump further insults these hardworking professionals by behaving recklessly with the information they give him, which he's supposed to protect. In May 2017, the president allegedly revealed highly classified information in an Oval Office meeting with Russia's foreign minister. The incident was detailed in a report by the *Washington Post*, which claimed Trump disclosed details about spying operations in Syria. As soon as the story hit, it spread like wildfire. "What the hell happened?" aides texted one another.

Intelligence officials—already on edge by the president's public comments—were mortified by the allegations. Whether the story was accurate or not, the fact that anyone thought it was plausible for the president of the United States to leak intelligence to an adversary says a great deal about the growing perception of the nation's chief executive. Only a few months earlier, Trump was caught on camera reviewing sensitive documents about North Korea on an open-air terrace at his Mar-a-Lago resort, using the light of cell phone screens (which of course have cameras on them) to read in the darkness alongside his visiting counterpart from Japan.

Trump's inept handling of intelligence was on display again one day when he flashed a peek at classified documents to a reporter at the White House. "See?" he said, holding up a fistful of papers and waving them as he tried to make a point about how in-the-know he was on world issues. "Many countries have given us great intelligence." Although the reporter couldn't see the content, the incident was discussed within the White House. The president has the authority to classify or declassify information as he wishes, so technically he could have shown the journalist whatever he wanted. Still, top National Security Council staff fretted about the president's carelessness, which they speculated could put secret programs in jeopardy.

The growing list of security lapses threatened a result more woeful than the exposure of "close hold" information. Some realized it could put people in danger, increasing the risk of harm to American citizens, and compromising the agents we recruit to collect such information—those who put their lives on the line to help America see around corners and anticipate new threats. According to press reports, agencies were forced to devise a plan to extract a high-level intelligence source from a hostile foreign country, partly out of fear that Trump's repeated disclosures might put the person in danger. Regardless of the veracity of the report, Trump's behavior certainly had a chilling effect throughout the national security community, making the already difficult jobs of those charged with safeguarding our country that much harder.

As if to outdo himself, the president tweeted a photo of a failed Iranian missile launch in summer 2019 to taunt Iran's government. The problem? The photo reportedly came from a US spy satellite and was shown to the president during a sensitive briefing. We were baffled. The "sources and methods" used to collect intelligence overseas are some of America's most closely guarded secrets, which Trump seemed to be putting at risk again out of ignorance or indifference. Former officials publicly voiced concerns that our adversaries could use the president's tweet to "reverse engineer" how the United States monitored the Iranian missile program, but it didn't take the skill of foreign adversaries. Within days, amateur researchers used the clues in the photograph to identify the alleged government satellite in the night sky that had taken the picture, which, if true, could allow those researchers to track it in the future.

Worse than his inability to keep a secret, Donald Trump is the ultimate "politicizer" of intelligence. Say what you want about George W. Bush and Dick Cheney leading the country to war by supposedly cherry-picking intelligence about Iraq. Their claims were at least based on real information collected at the time, backed by intelligence community analysts, and accepted by bipartisan majorities in Congress. Trump wants the information given to him to support his agenda, and he wants his intelligence officials to be "loyal," rather than to give it to him straight. This is the opposite of what our spy agencies should do. More than that, it's actually a threat to the security of the country because our commander in chief doesn't really care about the truth.

When intelligence professionals don't give him the assessments he wants, Trump attacks them. His biggest worry is when they appear in public or before Congress because he knows they will tell the truth. He doesn't want them sharing information that contradicts his views. On more than one occasion, the president has thought about removing an intelligence chief for offering a nonpartisan, impartial assessment to the American people's representatives in Congress.

I remember one day vividly. A top intelligence leader went up to testify on Capitol Hill. An official rang me at home late that evening.

"The president's red hot," she told me. "It sounds like he wants someone fired by morning."

"What the hell happened?" I asked.

She explained that the agency head offered an assessment about one of America's foreign adversaries. The conclusion was at odds with what Trump had been saying publicly. The intelligence was accurate; Trump just didn't like it. Someone in Congress must have asked the president about the discrepancy, tipping him off.

We scrambled to make sure Trump didn't take to Twitter to announce a new firing. Doing so, we argued, would make him look like he was trying to manipulate the intelligence process at a time when that would be very bad for him, especially with the Mueller investigation unfinished. Thankfully, he kept his powder dry, but only temporarily.

In January 2019, the president went ballistic after the heads of the Office of the Director of National Intelligence (DNI), CIA, FBI, and DIA testified in the Senate. They offered a number of blunt warnings that conflicted with the president's views, including that North Korea was unlikely to give up nuclear weapons and that ISIS was not defeated. The president went into a rage. An NFL linebacker couldn't have stopped him from getting on Twitter that day. "Perhaps Intelligence should go back to school!" he tweeted, blasting the "passive and naive" conclusions of his spy chiefs.

He wanted to fire them so badly, but he knew he couldn't. Instead, Trump summoned them to the Oval Office for a meeting, released a photo of the CIA and DNI heads seated around his desk, and declared they'd been "misquoted" on Capitol Hill. Their words were "taken out of context," he said. Trump tried to make it seem the spy chiefs came to repent, as if the information they'd testified about was wrong. It wasn't. And that's not at all what they told the president when the cameras were out of the room.

Meanwhile, back at the headquarters of those agencies, employees were dispirited to watch Trump (yet again) attack their work product. What's more, he was humiliating their bosses and using them as props to show that *he* was in charge and that *he* could control their findings. You'd think this would have been a weeks-long controversy in the intelligence community, but it wasn't. By that point, our intelligence professionals were so beaten down by the president's antics that they'd given up being outraged, though that didn't mean they'd lost a willingness to call out his misconduct. History has a way of restoring balance, and later in the year, it would be an intelligence community employee who would call out Trump for political double-dealing with his position and the subsequent White House cover-up.

The Oval Office meeting with the spy chiefs was one of the few occasions the president waited patiently to do what he really wanted to do in the heat of the moment. He sat on his hands. Then, several months later, he couldn't wait any longer and axed Director of National Intelligence Dan Coats and his deputy, Sue Gordon, pushing them out because they'd been too forthright about their analysis and too unwilling to become political mouthpieces. Trump wanted spy leaders who were more loyal, he told staff. He wouldn't hide his feelings, either. "We need somebody strong that can rein it in," the president told the media. "Because, as I think you've all learned, the intelligence agencies have run amok. They have run amok."

Trump decided to turn the tables. After enduring months of presidential pressure, the Justice Department began investigating the intelligence community and its findings about Russia and the 2016 election, which Trump had long disputed. The probe was described as "broad." The president could barely contain his glee. "This was treason. This was high crimes," Trump said of the work done by intelligence professionals. He wanted to do more than fire these Deep State traitors. He wanted to see them go to prison.

Tipping the Scales

The American judicial system was designed to straddle two branches. The executive branch investigates and prosecutes crimes, and the judicial branch determines guilt and innocence in the courts. The distinction is irrelevant to Trump. The president tries to browbeat the lawyers defending him, seeks to influence investigators investigating him, and attacks the judges judging him. As a result, he has undermined all aspects of the justice system in an effort to "tip the scales" in his favor.

When it comes to manipulating the system, Trump's first instinct is to force the answers he wants from his lawyers. He pressures them daily, and they feel the heat. He will berate them to their faces for not seeing the law the way he sees the law, and he cannot stand it when they tell him "No," which they incidentally have to do all the time. He presses them to get to "Yes" on issues where doing so would appear wholly inappropriate, even to the most uneducated listener. Trump tells agency heads to fire their lawyers and get new ones if they aren't getting the right results. If the American Bar Association could see it from the inside, they'd have a field day.

The president's former White House counsel, Don McGahn, had the backbone to stand up to Trump, which cannot be said of everyone. That's what is so concerning about his handling of government lawyers. Trump drives them to the edge of what's reasonable or legal and then badgers them until they take the plunge, bringing the administration along for the fall. It's an attitude that would be unworthy of a small-town mayor, and which is remarkably unbecoming for an American president.

We can tell when Trump is preparing to ask his lawyers to do something unethical or foolish because that's when he starts scanning the room for note takers.

"What the fuck are you doing?" he shouted at an aide who was scribbling in a notebook during a meeting. It's not uncommon for advisors to write down reminders during conversations with the president. How else are they supposed to record all of his marching orders?

The room went silent. The aide seemed confused about what was wrong.

"Are you fucking taking notes?" Trump continued, glaring.

"Uhh...sorry," the aide said, quietly closing the notebook and sitting up straighter in the chair.

His paranoia is the best evidence of a guilty conscience. After a particularly bad series of leaks from the White House, President Trump inquired about the possibility of surreptitiously monitoring the phones of White House staff. To avoid veering into "illegal" territory, staff interpreted this as the president asking for better "insider-threat detection" systems, a common practice in businesses or agencies working to prevent unauthorized disclosures. Here was a man who was apoplectic at the (completely false) theory that Barack Obama had his "wires tapped" at Trump Tower, but who was more than happy to tap those of the people around him.

The president won't let the cautiousness of government lawyers stop him from doing what he wants. If he really can't get the answers he demands, he seeks outside counsel, scouring the legal community for its unseemly members. He's found them in people such as longtime fixer Michael Cohen, whose loyalty to the president eventually faded when deeds on behalf of Trump landed him in legal hot water, and Rudy Giuliani, the disgraced former mayor of New York City. Few of us who interacted with Rudy over the years would have imagined that he would self-immolate so completely, but that is the inevitable consequence of traveling the globe (and the television networks) in defense of presidential corruption.

Trump's animus toward the law extends to judges and courts, too. He has less control over their actions, so he uses his bully pulpit to demean them and to question their legitimacy. Recall during the 2016 campaign when candidate Trump disparaged a judge for a ruling related to a lawsuit against Trump University by claiming the judge's Mexican heritage made him biased. At the time, CNN's Jake Tapper confronted Trump. "I don't care if you criticize him. That's fine. You can criticize every decision. What I'm saying is, if you invoke his race as a reason why he can't do his job—" "I think that's why he's doing it," Trump interrupted, doubling down and insisting the judge should recuse himself. The judge, by the way, was not from Mexico, but Indiana. Paul Ryan called it "the textbook definition of a racist comment."

After a ruling against the administration's immigration policies, President Trump blasted the court's decision as "a disgrace" and attacked the presiding judge as "an Obama judge" and said the court on which the man served was "really something we have to take a look at because it's not fair." Supreme Court Chief Justice John Roberts repudiated the president's attack, writing that the United States does not have "Obama judges or Trump judges, Bush judges or Clinton judges... The independent judiciary is something we should all be thankful for."

The president didn't let the comment slide. He went on a tweet storm, mocking the "independent judiciary" in quotations and suggesting the United States needed to break up the "complete & total disaster" Ninth Circuit Court of Appeals in order to start getting more favorable rulings for the Trump administration. His comments were liked by more than 100,000 people. In another outburst, the president assailed a judge for an injunction on his travel ban. "The opinion of this so-called judge, which essentially takes law-enforcement away from our country, is ridiculous and will be overturned!" He continued: "If something happens blame him and court system." This is the real threat. Trump may have perverse views of his own about justice, but he is exhorting others to share the opinion that US courts are corrupt and potentially a public danger, further corroding a key pillar of our democracy.

The president has proposed doing away with judges on more than one occasion. Too many of his policies are getting stuck in legal limbo, he says.

"Can we just *get rid* of the judges? Let's get rid of the fucking judges," Trump fumed one morning. "There shouldn't be any at all, really." He went a step further and asked his legal team to draft up a bill and send it to Congress to reduce the number of federal judges.

Staff ignored the outburst and the wacky request.

Trump continued complaining anyway. "I've only won *two* cases in the courts as president. And you know what one of them was? A case against a stripper."

Eyes widened at the reference. He would later repeat the comment, undoubtedly to get the same reaction from a new set of captive listeners.

The unavoidable conclusion is that the president sees himself as above the law, which is a scary point of view for a person who swears before God and the nation to "faithfully execute" it. The perception is evident by his almost mystical fascination with the power of the presidential pardon, which allows him to absolve convicted criminals of guilt. To Donald Trump, these are unlimited "Get Out of Jail Free" cards on a Monopoly board.

He has told officials that if they take illegal actions on his behalf, he will pardon them. Press outlets reported that the president once offered pardons for his wall-builders, urging them to ignore regulations standing in the way of his precious barrier and to plow ahead, regardless of the consequences. He'd have their backs, pardon in hand, if they got into legal trouble. Spokespeople were immediately dispatched to pour cold water on the reporting. Tellingly, they didn't deny what the president said but insisted his comments were made in jest. Once again, for the record, that's how you know Donald Trump is not joking—when he sends someone out to say that he was joking.

Trump has also claimed he can pardon himself, if needed. He tweeted in June 2018, "...I have the absolute right to PARDON myself, but why would I do that when I have done nothing wrong?" The comment eerily paralleled Nixon's statement: "If the president does it, it's not illegal." Ask yourself, are these the words of a man who's planning to follow the law? In a sad way, it's almost a relief when he makes these statements, because it allows the public to see what advisors are experiencing every day behind the curtain, without the president labeling it as "fake news" from anonymous sources.

Trump reserves a special place in his heart for our last category of the justice system: investigators. It's essential in a democracy that those who investigate crimes be impartial, that their inquiries are not tainted by outside influence. Yet there is nothing that makes the president's head explode like the prospect of being investigated, as America witnessed during Trump's up-all-night, burn-it-down obsession with what he famously labeled "THE WITCH HUNT." The Mueller Report revealed the lengths to which the president will go to interfere with the investigative process. Before you even dive into the text, the executive summary notes that his conduct involved "public attacks on the investigation, non-public efforts to control it, and efforts in both public and private to encourage witnesses not to cooperate with the investigation."

You could make the case that the Mueller ordeal wouldn't have happened in the first place if the president had restrained himself from trying to influence the Russia probe. On May 9, 2017, the president fired FBI director Jim Comey. He sent the director a termination letter that said the attorney general and deputy attorney general had recommended to him that Comey be dismissed. "I have accepted their recommendation and you are hereby terminated and removed from office, effective immediately," the president wrote. "While I greatly appreciate you informing me, on three separate occasions, that I am not under investigation, I nevertheless concur with the judgment of the Department of Justice that you are not able to effectively lead the Bureau." He closed with: "I wish you the best of luck in your future endeavors."

It would be an understatement to say that people around him were both pissed off and spooked at what appeared to be Trump's attempt to protect himself from being investigated. Here, Trump fanboys will throw up a red flag. "Come on," they might say, "the president fired Comey because the man lost the public trust by grandstanding. Even Clinton was happy." What those supporters didn't see, though, was how fast the Washington, DC, switchboards melted down that afternoon, as the president's advisors called one another with concerned speculation about his action. None of us really believed he was trying to "do what was right."

Not long after, the president's justification began to unravel. While he claimed he made the decision at the advice of the Justice Department's two top officials, Trump's own explanations in the ensuing days contradicted this. In an interview with NBC News, he cited the Russia probe as one of the reasons he had gotten rid of Comey. "I said to myself, I said, 'You know, this Russia thing with Trump and Russia is a made-up story,'" he told the outlet. The same month in a meeting with Russian officials at the White House, the president confessed to them that dismissing Jim had relieved "great pressure." It was soon revealed that the president had actually asked the Justice Department to draft the firing recommendation that was given to him, which they did reluctantly. It was all staged.

The president's sudden firing of the FBI director—and then the shifting explanations—were seen within his own White House as a dangerous move that could set in motion a series of events the result of which might be the downfall of the administration. At least one cabinet member mulled resigning. "I'm genuinely worried for the country," the official confessed, although apparently not worried enough to make the point publicly. Officials held their breath, and it only got grimmer.

Trump became unhinged when Rod Rosenstein, the Justice Department's number two, made the decision on May 19 to launch an independent investigation into Russian interference. Rosenstein appointed former FBI director Bob Mueller as "special counsel" to lead the probe. We all watched with a sense of doom as Trump soon began searching for ways to get rid of Mueller. Within days of Comey's firing, he argued that the special counsel needed to go because he was "conflicted," contending that Mueller was a Never-Trumper, wanted to be named FBI director again, and had a Trump golf course membership. But aides told President Trump the "conflicts" were imagined, and they feared his demand was meant to impede the investigation.

One day in June, I got a message from an administration colleague who was watching an outside Trump surrogate make the media rounds suggesting the president might be getting ready to fire Mueller. The surrogate wouldn't have said this if Trump hadn't spoken to him.

"Man oh man, what the fuck is he doing?" my colleague lamented.

"You got me," I responded. If firing Comey hadn't toppled the administration, firing Bob Mueller absolutely would. How was this not obvious to Trump? I assumed his white-hot anger was blinding him to the fact that he was putting his presidency on the line.

Trump privately told White House counsel Don McGahn that he needed to have Rod Rosenstein get rid of the special counsel. No way, McGahn warned. "Knocking out Mueller," he said, would be "another fact used to claim" that Trump had committed obstruction of justice, according to the investigation's final report. The president tried again on June 17, 2017, phoning McGahn from Camp David. "You gotta do this," he insisted. "You gotta call Rod." Trump reiterated the order the next day. McGahn ignored both requests and threatened to resign. When the story broke, the president told Don to dispute it and to "create a record stating he had not been ordered to have the special counsel removed." McGahn refused to lie, and the president called him into the Oval Office to pressure him, an entreaty his chief lawyer again rebuffed.

After the Mueller Report dropped, hundreds of former federal prosecutors signed a letter stating that Trump's efforts to derail the investigation constituted obstruction of justice. He would have faced "multiple felony charges" if he weren't president of the United States, they said. Some of these signers were left-wing pundits as you'd expect, but others served in Republican administrations, including Jeffrey Harris, a former Justice Department attorney under Ronald Reagan and a friend of Rudy Giuliani. "Whether to prosecute this kind of conduct was not a close prosecutorial call," Harris told one newspaper when asked about signing the statement. "This was a no-brainer." I'll leave that conclusion to others, but at a bare minimum, episodes like the one with McGahn are entirely inexcusable for a US leader.

One of the biggest casualties of the Mueller saga was the FBI. The agents that work in the Hoover Building, its headquarters, have no other motive than to serve their country and root out the truth. I've seen their work up close. Yet they've received a merciless, ongoing beating from the president. Many of these investigators quietly cheered for candidate Donald Trump outside of work, and now they can't believe the man who tells law enforcement he'll "have their backs" is stabbing them in theirs, regularly. The FBI director has tried to stand up for his workforce, saying in response to presidential criticism, "The opinions I care about are the opinions of the people who actually know us through our work." It's not enough to counter Trump's megaphone.

The president claims the bureau is an untrustworthy breeding ground of Deep-State conspirators. Over and over again, he calls the FBI "crooked" and disparages its employees. "Tremendous leaking, lying and corruption at the highest levels," "a tool of anti-Trump political actors," "politicized the sacred investigative process," "tainted," "very dishonest," "worst in history," "its reputation in tatters." Never has an American president taken aim so often, at so many people, for such terrible reasons. Not enough folks around Trump have pushed back and told him to cut the crap, so the president continues pummeling another democratic institution unabated.

The result is that millions of Americans now have an excuse to doubt the conclusions of the nation's premier law enforcement agency. Trump's broadsides against the FBI are inspiring commentators to politicize the bureau's activities and invent conspiracy theories, as Fox News host Tucker Carlson did not long ago when he ridiculed the FBI's warnings about the rise of white nationalist violence as "a hoax." Tell that to the families who've lost loved ones to racially motivated mass shootings.

Oversight in the Dark

Donald Trump's attacks on the executive branch and the judicial branch leave one other institution to check his power—the United States Congress. The authorities of the legislative branch are enumerated in the Constitution in Article I, before all others. The ordering was intentional. The Founders believed Congress was the closest to the people. It was the body of their representatives, who were chosen more frequently than any other branch of government, and although all three were meant to be co-equal, if any branch had primacy, it was meant to be the legislative.

The US Congress has been a persistent irritant to our nation's chief executive, even when both chambers—the House and Senate—were controlled by Republicans. It's clear to anyone who's ever had a serious discussion with the president about the legislative process that he has no idea how it works, or is supposed to work. Senate traditions, such as the filibuster, mean nothing to him, and he finds it farcical that congressional committees have authority to oversee his agencies. He is forced to re-learn daily that it's necessary to build bipartisan consensus to get anything substantial accomplished, and then he promptly forgets.

Now more than ever is an appropriate time for Congress to play its watchdog role. The president knows this, too, which is why he has sought to further diminish public support for the body by deflecting criticism onto US representatives and senators for his own failings, sneering at the dictates of the legislative branch, and actively obstructing congressional oversight of his administration.

The president is grateful to have other politicians to blame. When he didn't get the first budget deal he wanted? The fault went to the Republican-controlled Congress. When he didn't get the second budget deal he wanted? The still-Republican-controlled Congress. The third time around? Congress, this time run by the Democrats. Factories closing in America? "Get smart Congress!" Immigration? "Congress, fund the WALL!" Caring for our nation's veterans? "Congress must fix." The failure to reform health care? "Congress must pass a STRONG law." Children dying in homeland security's custody? "Any deaths of children or others at the Border are strictly the fault of the Democrats." You get the picture.

Congress is an easy target because it doesn't move very fast. This is partly by constitutional design. The architects of our nation wanted all sides to come together when there were *shared* interests, and they wanted to avoid a thin majority being able to steamroll everyone else. That's why Trump told us to hire him, right? He said he could cut good deals; he was better at it than anyone in the world. Yet for a man who built a reputation on negotiating, Trump turned out to be a pretty terrible dealmaker. His record of bringing everyone together on Capitol Hill is dismal. That's why he's forced to declare emergencies, on matters ranging from the border to foreign policy, which allows him to take actions which he knows would never be supported by bipartisan majorities. He spends more time posting snarky messages about members of Congress than trying to build support for his agenda, preferring a good schoolyard spat over the hard work of legislating. Consequently, his congressional-relations aides are in a perpetual state of consternation.

Increasingly, Trump has decided to ignore Congress altogether. He's told advisors to do the same, goading them to flagrantly defy congressional restrictions. One time, a leader of a national security agency asked the president for support in convincing Congress to pass an upcoming defense bill. Trump could use his megaphone to prod representatives who were on the fence to support the legislation.

"Don't worry about Congress," the president said. "Just do what you need to do."

The official explained that it wasn't like that. The law needed to pass so that certain defense restrictions could be lifted. Until then, the agency wouldn't be able to do its job to protect the American people. That's why they needed Trump to champion passage of the bill.

"No, no. It doesn't matter. You have my permission to do whatever you need to do, okay? Just forget about them."

The official sat in stunned silence and then gave up, moving on to the next topic.

Donald Trump is also comfortable flouting Congress when the law explicitly says Congress *shouldn't* be ignored, *should* be consulted, or *must* approve something before action can be taken.

He infuriated Capitol Hill by moving forward with controversial weapons sales to Saudi Arabia and the United Arab Emirates without congressional permission. By law, the president is required to provide Congress a thirty-day heads-up before weapons sales can move forward, allowing them an opportunity to block the transactions. Trump knew there was bipartisan opposition, so he invoked an "emergency" provision in the law, sent it to Congress at the last minute, and went forward with the sales anyway. To be clear, there was no "emergency," and Trump set another bad precedent for future chief executives to pretend the legislative branch doesn't matter.

The president hasn't tried to hide the fact that he actively shuns Congress's crucial "human resources" role. The Constitution requires the president to nominate the government's senior-most leaders and to appoint them to their positions only "with the advice and consent of the Senate." But Trump prefers to keep *un-nominated* and *un-confirmed* individuals in key posts, as noted earlier by his own admission. It's off-putting to watch how agency heads must continuously curry his favor and carry out his bidding if they hope to ever be nominated, and thus, they are more loyal to him and less accountable to Congress. All told, midway through his third year, Trump had nearly 1,400 cumulative days of cabinet vacancies in his administration, days when top agencies had no confirmed leader. By comparison, Barack Obama had 288 cabinet vacancy days at the same point, and George W. Bush only 34.

The gaps mean Congress only has a temporary official to hold accountable. "Acting" leaders are more like babysitters than empowered executives, and are often hesitant to wade into congressional waters until an actual top official is named. Legislative requests get put "on hold." Hearings get delayed. Transparency weakens. When the organs of state lurch along for months like this, rudderless and without robust congressional monitoring, the functions of government atrophy. The potential for abuse grows, and the end result is bad for organizational management and bad for democracy.

On top of it all, the president has fought to actively obstruct legislative inquiries. It's become almost a regular occurrence for him to snub congressional requests and even subpoenas, which are supposed to be Capitol Hill's most powerful weapon to compel information from the executive branch. Trump now treats these official demands like junk mail. He has his lawyers dismiss them by flaunting "executive privilege," the prerogative of a president to prevent the disclosure of certain confidential information and advice. The refusals go beyond standard practice and have turned into a full block-and-tackle exercise against congressional investigators across an array of Trump administration controversies. The president himself admits as

much to this subversion of proper legislative oversight, having declared categorically that the administration will be "fighting all the subpoenas" from
Congress and daring the legislative branch to do
something about it.

Frankly, this makes it a lot harder to promote
the president's policies when we go up to Capitol
Hill. Members of Congress don't want to listen to
us if we won't listen to them. Meetings these days
start off with a list of grievances. Behind closed
doors, senators and congressmen rattle off all the
ways our administration has undercut their man-
dates or flat-out ignored them, and I'm not just
talking about Democrats. I've gotten the same
treatment from Republicans, too. We're forced to
tell these representatives that our hands are tied
until the president changes his mind or they have
something to trade with him.

The obstruction is part of a deliberate and coordinated campaign. Before the midterm elections,
the White House counsel's office started developing a contingency plan to shield the executive
branch in case Democrats took power. New lawyers were brought in, and new procedures were
put in place. The goal wasn't just to prepare for a
barrage of legislative requests. It was a concerted
attempt to fend off congressional oversight. When

Democrats finally took the House, the unspoken administration policy toward Capitol Hill became: Give as little as possible, wait as long as possible. Even routine inquiries are now routed to the lawyers, who have found unique ways to say "We can't right now," "Give us a few months," "We're going to need to put you on hold," "Probably not," "No," and "Not a chance in hell."

Of course it must be said that no one here is blameless. The Democrats came into power with uncontrolled anger toward Donald Trump and an attitude that the ends justified the means, as long as it brought him down. They told their base they would investigate anything and everything that moved, which is a particularly stupid tone to strike when your hope is to get the executive branch to cooperate with a probe, if only initially. A number of House investigations are obviously political in nature and lack substance. At the same time, others are the legitimate duty of Congress, from examining executive branch ethics violations to analyzing whether official government actions were taken for political purposes.

It's not the White House's job to decide what Congress should oversee. That decision was made centuries ago and effectively enshrined in the Constitution. Congress is a co-equal branch of government, and one of its many rightful roles is to monitor the executive. The more vehemently the president inhibits that proper function, the more likely future administrations will avoid account-ability, creating fresh opportunities for government malpractice.

A common refrain you hear in the Trump adminis-tration after the president cooks up an unwelcome scheme is "We'll get enjoined by the courts imme-diately." His ideas veer toward impropriety and illegality so often that virtually every senior official has heard this phrase, said this phrase, or fears this phrase. It's the canary in the coal mine—the signal that a bad idea is about to come crashing down. Donald Trump is the miner with his headphones on and the music turned up, oblivious to the warn-ings. Sometimes it seems he genuinely enjoys tak-ing actions that will get the administration sued.

While we were on the road one day, a fellow advisor vented about a request issued from the Oval Office. Trump wanted to use a domestic presiden-tial power to do something absurd overseas, which for security reasons I cannot disclose.

"It doesn't make sense. So I told him he doesn't understand. We're talking about apples and refrigerators here," the official remarked. "He doesn't get it. He just doesn't get it. Also, if we do any of this stuff, we'll get enjoined by the courts right away."

The phrase stayed in my head. Apples and refrigerators. When the president mixes up words, the result is unusual; when he mixes up concepts, the result can be unlawful. It's like the time Trump told ABC's George Stephanopoulos that he would consider accepting dirt from a foreign government, such as China or Russia, about a political opponent. The president said he would take it, equating the information to opposition research, or "oppo research." To Trump, it would be mere politics. To some experts, it would be "textbook illegal." Hadn't the special counsel just finished investigating whether this happened in 2016? How could President Trump, after that national nightmare, still not understand the difference between politics-as-usual and naked corruption? Didn't he care? The ABC interview foreshadowed the answer. No, he didn't.

Only months later, Trump decided to use the influence of the presidency to pressure Ukraine to investigate one of his potential 2020 election rivals. He urged the country's president to launch an inquiry into Joe Biden and his son, Hunter, whose profitable work for a Ukrainian gas company drew scrutiny, especially in light of his father's engagement with Ukraine as vice president. Whether or not the allegation of improper dealings had merit, the system was not supposed to work this way. It's up to the Justice Department to probe potential crimes. American presidents don't implore foreign leaders to open investigations into domestic political opponents. But with the campaign consuming his daily mental bandwidth, Trump couldn't resist the temptation to use his office to gain a competitive edge.

Those of us who have seen these sorts of reckless actions, again and again, wanted to slam our heads against the wall. The explanation that he wanted to help combat "corruption" in Ukraine was barely believable to anyone around him. The obvious corruption was in the Oval Office. The president had apparently learned nothing from the Mueller saga. Only we did. We learned that, given enough time and space, Donald J. Trump will seek to abuse any power he is given. This is a fact of life we've been taught inside his administration through repeated example. No external force can ameliorate his attraction to wrongdoing. His presidency is continually jeopardized by it, and so are America's institutions.

If the president's assault on democracy seems too remote for most Americans, don't worry. You can look closer to home because President Trump has sought to abuse his power to target you directly. He has repeatedly tried to leverage his office to punish what he calls "Democratic states"—those where the majority of citizens voted for Hillary Clinton in 2016, ignoring the fact that his supporters live in those places, as well. The president surprises staff with horrifying ways to make life difficult for these parts of America.

California is the quintessential example. Trump hates California. He can't believe that an entertainer such as himself is unable to win over the home of Hollywood. He rants about its governor, Gavin Newsom, for criticizing administration policies, and he believes the state "stole" electoral votes from him by allowing so many supposed "illegal" voters to cast ballots. After wildfires devastated homes and properties in California, Trump insisted that federal funds be cut off to the state. No emergency dollars should be flowing to Californians, the president told staff. Word of his spiteful demand spread throughout the building, in part because Trump was raising the idea, as he often did, with random people. It was jaw-dropping, especially considering that clips of burned-out homes and Americans living in temporary shelters were still replaying on our television screens.

To protect the president from himself, staff members tried to make sure the press didn't get a hold of the story. Communications aides breathed a sigh of relief when it seemed the storm had passed. Then several weeks later, the president fired off tweets anyway, saying he'd ordered relief aid for California to be halted, probably because he was frustrated that it hadn't. To my knowledge, officials never acted on the public demand. It faded from view. But the request showed his true colors, as a politician blatantly seeking to hurt people in places where he can't see an electoral advantage.

He's found other ways to go after the state, though. President Trump announced that the administration was revoking California's tailpipe emissions waiver, which for years allowed the state to set a tougher standard when it came to reducing automobile pollution. He's moved to cut funding for its high-speed rail projects, and he's threatened to dump more migrants in California to punish it for statewide policies shielding illegal immigrants, only a sample from a longer list. If Congress is examining politically motivated activity in the Executive Branch, might I suggest that some of these threats and decisions warrant further scrutiny.

The net effect of the president's war on demo-

cratic institutions is that he has turned the government of the United States into one of his companies:
a badly managed enterprise defined by a socio-
pathic personality in the c-suite, rife with infighting, embroiled in lawsuits, falling deeper into debt,
allergic to internal and external criticism, open to
shady side deals, operating with limited oversight,
and servicing its self-absorbed owner at the expense
of its customers. We should have seen this one coming. This is only what President Trump has done
here at home. Remember, this man is also the de-
facto leader of the free world.

CHAPTER 5

A Weakness for Strongmen

"Let every nation know, whether it wishes us well or ill, that we shall pay any price, bear any burden, meet any hardship, support any friend, oppose any foe to assure the survival and success of liberty."

—*John F. Kennedy*

L GBT...Q...I...ZXW?—who knows," one Trump official laughed, trying to spell out the abbreviation used to define aspects of sexuality and gender. "I just learned what the *I* stood for."

"Interracial?" another interjected.

"No. *Intersex*," the first explained. "I still don't know what the hell that actually means, though." More laughter.

This was a group of senior Trump officials chatting about the president's participation in a G7 summit. The Group of Seven ("G7") consists of the world's wealthiest nations, comprised of the United States, Canada, France, Germany, Italy, Japan, and the United Kingdom, which gather regularly to discuss economic and security issues. In June 2018, Canada was set to play host to the annual get-together of leaders. The Canadians announced that gender equality and women's empowerment would be a major focus, among other issues, and several officials mused about whether sexual orientation might come up, too. It was not the agenda they were hoping for.

Some White House aides were not taking the gathering seriously in part because the president himself wasn't taking it seriously. Trump didn't like forums where he wasn't guaranteed star billing, or where he would be outnumbered by other leaders with different points of view. He was never one to sit through long meetings, and most of the issues that concerned our allies didn't interest him. Additionally, in advance of the summit, Trump alienated—or was in the process of alienating—a majority of the G7 allies. He'd recently slapped tariffs on a number of them and was being criticized by the group, which has historically worked to break down trade barriers, not erect new ones. The president considered pulling out, but it was impossible to come up with a suitable excuse for stiffing America's biggest allies.

Trump faced two options. He could take the criticism in stride and steer the conversation at the G7 toward issues that could unite the allies. Or he could play the role of sore loser and sow deeper division. None of us were surprised when he veered toward the latter. Advisors braced for the summit to be a failure before Air Force One ever left Washington.

The prediction that the event was going to be "bad" became a self-fulfilling prophecy. The hosts were upset when the president arrived late. Trump berated other leaders about "unfair trade practices." He grew irritated with Japanese prime minister Shinzō Abe, at one point apparently telling him in a meeting: "Shinzō, you don't have this problem [of illegal immigration], but I can send you twenty-five million Mexicans and you'll be out of office very soon." He tossed Starburst candy at German chancellor Angela Merkel, remarking, "Here, Angela. Don't say I never give you anything." And then he left the summit early, rounding off the visit with a tweetstorm blasting Canadian prime minister Justin Trudeau as "so meek and mild…very dishonest & weak," and announcing that the United States was backing out of the joint statement signed only hours earlier with the other leaders.

What a horrible mess, I thought. This isn't how we'd act toward our enemies at an international summit, and these were our close friends. Not only that, we'd wasted an opportunity to show solidarity with them on important issues where we had common interests. Perhaps worst of all, the president alarmed everyone at the summit by publicly calling for a nation-state rival, Russia, to be readmitted into the G7 meetings. Russia had been cast out of the group over its invasion of Crimea. Since then, Vladimir Putin had done little to demonstrate he was a responsible world partner, but the president questioned why the allies should meet at all if Moscow wasn't invited. It was as if Putin himself had written Trump's talking points.

In any event, Trump didn't care about the tiny trail of destruction he left on the way out of Canada. His mind was elsewhere. He was flying to make *new* friends, on the other side of the world. The G7 was merely a distraction standing in the way of the month's main event: his meeting with Kim Jong Un, the brutal dictator of North Korea. Trump would later reveal it was the meeting where he and Kim "fell in love."

National security is the most important responsibility of the commander in chief. He must protect the American people against external threats and provide for the safety and security of the nation. Everything else is secondary to this charge. The primary domain for achieving lasting security is in foreign policy. That's where the president must have clear-cut plans to keep our extended neighborhood safe by working closely with like-minded allies and keeping dangerous adversaries at arm's length.

President Trump doesn't see the world this way. It's never been fully clear to me why, but he's flipped the script, distancing himself from America's friends and courting its foes. He regularly discards the advice of seasoned foreign policy professionals in the administration. He has struggled to develop a coherent security strategy, leaving "America First" open to interpretation and changing his mind on consequential decisions without warning. Worst of all, he has seemingly abandoned a century-long consensus about America's role as leader of the free world.

Empire of Liberty

To put President Trump's foreign policy into context, it's important to understand history. Prior to the twentieth century, we are taught, the United States was an isolationist country. In his farewell address, George Washington said it was America's policy to "steer clear" of foreign entanglements. John Quincy Adams declared twenty-five years later that the United States was not a nation that went "abroad in search of monsters to destroy." America didn't become an assertive country, the story goes, until it boldly intervened in the First World War and turned the tide against fascism. This is an oversimplistic rendering.

Since its earliest days, the United States has been an expansionist nation, focused on shaping international developments. The Founding Fathers predicted their young republic would become a strong country, if not the world's strongest. In the same speech quoted above, President Washington outlined a vision for America to be mighty enough "to bid defiance to any power on earth." The other Founders shared his aim and believed the United States was a "Hercules in a cradle," destined one day to flex its muscles globally and create an "empire of liberty." In the short term, those ambitions were tempered by the need to build the country's institutions to a competitive level, but once it gained the requisite strength, the United States began spreading its ideals in far-off places.

The continuous effort to shape a more democratic world became a unifying theme, even as the White House changed hands. Historians note that nearly every president in the last hundred years embraced this foreign-policy consensus. Democrat Woodrow Wilson vowed that America would stand for "the principles of a liberated mankind...whether in war or in peace." Republican Dwight Eisenhower said the country would strive to strengthen the "special bonds" between free people "the world over." While some presidents were more hawkish than others about reinforcing democracies overseas, variations of the same theme were carried forward from Kennedy to Obama.

Donald Trump is the clear outlier. After getting sworn in, he took shots at his predecessors' foreign adventurism. "For many decades," he said, "we've...subsidized the armies of other countries while allowing for the very sad depletion of our military; we've defended other nations' borders while refusing to defend our own; and spent trillions of dollars overseas while America's infrastructure has fallen into disrepair and decay. We've made other countries rich while the wealth, strength, and confidence of our country has disappeared over the horizon." It was a call to pull back and look inward.

Each of Trump's claims are false and his attempted point is based on a short-sighted view of history. We would be far worse off today if the United States hadn't invested in the success of our friends. America would be poorer and less secure, struggling to fend off hostile countries in a more menacing global neighborhood. Instead, we played an active role in the world, which went from being composed almost entirely of dictatorships and monarchies to being majority democratic thanks to our efforts. This opened markets for our goods, facilitated the spread of knowledge, and gave us new partners who would have our backs in times of trouble.

America's dominant role on the international stage is at risk today. Rising nations are trying to compete against the United States. Henry Kissinger forecast this development a quarter century ago, predicting that in our time America would "be the greatest and most powerful nation, but a nation with peers." Kissinger argued that the emergence of rivals should not be seen as a "symptom of national decline." It's not proof that we overextended ourselves, as Trump says. Competition is a fact of life. Kissinger noted that for most of its existence the United States was not the sole superpower, so "the rise of other power centers" shouldn't surprise us. We should be concerned, however, if those rivals do not share our values and try to deconstruct the world America built.

Our response at such a pivotal moment must be to *fortify* our position. We should be deepening relationships with allies. We should be fighting forward with our principles. For every step we take backward, adversaries will step forward on the world stage to accomplish their priorities instead of ours. Unfortunately, my experience serving under this president has left me convinced Trump is shifting America into reverse. He's not positioning us to strengthen our empire of liberty. Instead he's left the empire's flank vulnerable to power-hungry competitors.

"More Unpredictable"

Candidate Donald Trump outlined his foreign policy views in detail for the first time on April 27, 2016. He attached a bumper sticker, "America First," to his plans for international engagement, declaring it would be "the major and overriding theme of my administration." Whether he intended to or not, Trump borrowed a longtime isolationist motto, which had been used by individuals opposed to US involvement in the Second World War. It was fitting because his America First plan was isolationist in spirit.

His comments became quite revealing later in the speech. "We must as a nation be more unpredictable," he told the audience. "We tell everything. We're sending troops. We tell them. We're sending something else. We have a news conference. We have to be unpredictable. And we have to be unpredictable starting now." The exhortation turned out to be the best encapsulation of Trump's foreign policy: *unpredictability*. It's a natural carryover of the president's governing philosophy, which as we've discussed is characterized by careless spontaneity. The president likes to keep everyone guessing about his views, sometimes even himself, but the stakes are much higher in foreign policy than they are on talk shows or Twitter.

After the president was sworn in, the national security team took longer than usual to coalesce. Most incoming officials were not on the campaign, did not know Trump, and were in many cases unfamiliar with one another. For secretary of state, he chose Rex Tillerson, the former head of Exxon, and General Jim Mattis as secretary of defense. The choices were notable because the two men, both with extensive international experience, did not share Trump's isolationist, what's-in-it-for-me attitude toward the world. It became evident that he chose Jim and Rex less because he wanted people who would challenge him and more because he thought their résumés would make him look good. He got the head of the world's biggest company to work for him, *and* one of America's most acclaimed generals! That's how he characterized it to confidants.

The national security advisor is supposed to sit at the center of the team. Not as a co-equal, but as an honest broker. This person must be the central nervous system, connecting the president at the head with the arms and legs, which provide feedback and carry out his orders. President Trump's first national security advisor, Mike Flynn, didn't quite fit the bill. He lasted several weeks before he was ousted for making misleading statements about contacts with the Russians. Those who'd spent any time with Flynn knew he had weird views on international issues and didn't show great judgment, so the change was for the better.

The bumpy beginning—a team that didn't really know one another and aides getting fired—meant no one was really "in charge." The president didn't have a strong national-security crew to bring along with him from the campaign because he didn't think he needed one. He was his own best advisor. But all of a sudden Trump was responsible for the most powerful nation on earth. What if a real crisis happened? A top Republican on Capitol Hill reached out to express concern. "It looks like there aren't hands on the wheel of the car yet," he said to me. "The administration needs to get its act together fast." I agreed.

Flynn was replaced by General H. R. McMaster, another celebrated military leader, who recognized the disjointedness of the president's security team. He resolved to bring order. H. R. saw his mandate clearly. He was supposed to bring the players to the table and execute the president's vision; soon he was hosting weekly conference calls with White House staff and agency heads. The goal was to keep everyone on the same page on foreign policy, but a recurring problem emerged. No one knew what page the president was on. Or if he was even reading from the same book.

All folks knew was that Trump was living up to his word on using "unpredictability" as a guiding principle. One minute, he might try to jettison a longstanding free trade agreement after a bad phone call with the Canadian president, and the next he might propose cutting off a US lifeline to a stalwart ally because he thought it was costing too much. Everyone developed policy whiplash, from advisors a stone's throw beyond the Oval Office to ambassadors stationed abroad. What was going on inside Trump's head? We had no idea what he'd do next, and it wasn't obvious the president did either. Decisions were made by the seat of his pants. Those privy to the content of the president's phone calls with foreign leaders were red-faced with embarrassment. To us, he came off like a complete amateur, using important calls to brag about himself and make awkward comments.

US allies felt the same way. His strange proclamations and irascibility shocked them. Behind the scenes, they begged us—fruitlessly—to get him to stop tweeting. "Please," one foreign leader implored, "you must get him off of Twitter. It's hurting the relationship." His country had been in the crosshairs of a recent Trump missive, and he argued that he couldn't be seen by his people working with the United States if the president was going to blast them all the time. We agreed, but assured him it was a lost cause. Trump's social media addiction was unmanageable.

The volume of tweets-turned-crises abroad grew weekly. More than a year into the first term, members of the foreign policy team were huddling on such an issue. Trump's social-media missives were limiting US response options to an overseas incident, the full details of which will not be released for some years. A new hire on the team was visibly frustrated. "The president needs to stop tweeting!" he said with exasperation, insinuating that we all should have confronted the bad habit sooner. "Wow, we never thought of that before," a veteran agency head quipped in response. The official was getting a hands-on lesson in what the rest of us already knew by then—that we were captive to the haphazardness.

We found out fast that the president couldn't articulate how he wanted to prioritize his foreign policy goals. The NSC tried to address his lack of strategic direction by giving him one. As required by law, the president must produce a security "strategy" for America. H. R. hoped he could work with Trump on developing a plan for international engagement, getting him away from reactive decision-making. He had staff put together a paper extolling the importance of US alliances, hailing post-war institutions like NATO, and calling for tougher action against rivals like Russia and North Korea. The presumption was naive. The president didn't care, and he didn't read the lengthy public document, which became more of a discarded homework assignment than a guide for US policy.

If the president's closest advisors cannot anticipate his next move, then everyone else is really in the dark. The agencies the commander in chief relies on to implement his policies are left directionless, and allies are likewise unable to coordinate with us effectively. Sure, uncertainty can keep foreign enemies on their toes, but after a while, they stop taking you seriously, which is what is happening to Trump. He's the international equivalent of the "boy who cried wolf": Friends and foes alike are writing him off. The last words you want to hear about your president from a foreign official are, "Yeah, we do our best not to pay attention." Regrettably, that's what they're saying.

Trump assailed Barack Obama during the

presidential campaign for a decline in US global leadership. It would *not* happen on his watch, he said. In the "America First" speech, then-candidate Trump told the audience that "our friends are beginning to think they can't depend on us" because of Obama's eight years of retrenchment. "We've had a president who dislikes our friends and bows to our enemies, something that we've never seen before in the history of our country...The truth is they don't respect us." Trump said he'd change direction, but if such a trend existed under the Obama administration, he seems to have doubled down on it.

Blinded by the Might

Donald Trump scoffed at President Obama's outreach to dictators. In 2011, he derided the president for catering to the authoritarian Chinese regime with "pretty please" diplomacy. In 2012, he blasted Obama for "bowing to the Saudi king." In 2013, he mocked the president's trip to the notoriously repressive Cuban island to meet Raul Castro. In 2014, he said Obama was foolish for calling Russia a "regional power," for telling the Russians he would have more flexibility after his re-election, and for letting Putin reemerge on the world stage.

As president of the United States, Trump has shown a far greater affinity for "strongmen" than Obama ever did. Historically, our nation's chief executives have chosen their words carefully when talking about dictatorial foreign leaders to avoid giving them more credibility than they deserve. Trump, by contrast, lavishes them with praise. Whether he is applauding Philippine president Rodrigo Duterte for his "unbelievable job" cracking down on drugs (a crackdown partly carried out by murdering suspects without a trial) or hailing authoritarian Turkish president Recep Erdoğan as a "friend" whom he is "very close to" (Erdoğan has launched sweeping efforts to jail political opponents and critics), Trump has a soft spot for tough guys.

Saudi Arabia is a prime example. After the brutal murder of *Washington Post* columnist Jamal Khashoggi at the hands of Saudi hitmen in October 2018, the president struggled to bring himself to criticize the regime's leadership. Even after intelligence community assessments reportedly pegged ultimate blame for the state-sponsored assassination on Saudi crown prince Mohammed bin Salman, Trump didn't want to condemn a man in whom he'd previously expressed "great confidence." "I want to stick with an ally that in many ways has been very good," the president told reporters, adding that the Saudi leader had denied involvement in the Khashoggi murder anyway, which seemed good enough for him.

The president acknowledged it was clearly the "worst cover-up of all time," but he liked the crown prince. He liked him a lot. And he didn't want to get on the Saudis' bad side. "I am not going to talk about this anymore!" he vented to lieutenants. "Oil is at fifty dollars a barrel. Do you know how stupid it would be to pick this fight? Oil would go up to one hundred fifty dollars a barrel. Jesus. How fucking stupid would I be?" We really hoped the president wouldn't go public with that explanation for staying silent. Then he did. Rather than criticize his friend the crown prince, Trump openly thanked him for keeping oil prices low, then later told reporters it was a reason he wouldn't break with the Saudis.

He may also have been influenced by his son-in-law, Jared, who'd struck up a friendship with the crown prince. Following the killing, Jared was messaging Mohammed bin Salman and urged anyone who would listen to withhold judgment. "You've got to see it from his perspective," he told administration colleagues. "He makes a point— 'My neighborhood is more dangerous than yours. I have Yemen. I have Iran. I have Syria.' And he's right!" Jared said with a laugh. "Can you imagine if we had something like Yemen at our southern border instead of Mexico? We'd be acting differently." An appalled staff member on the other end of the exchange relayed it to others in the West Wing. Jared's insinuation was that if we were in Saudi shoes, we'd murder journalists, too. NSC leaders were nonplussed.

The Khashoggi episode—made worse by weeks of presidential hand-wringing—damaged America's credibility, yet it was hardly the worst case of the president's submission to autocrats. That honor goes to Vladimir Putin. Under President Putin, Russia has reasserted itself on the world stage, challenging the United States at every opportunity and seeking to be a peer competitor. Trump, seemingly unfazed by the regime's hostility toward Americans, has applauded Putin with regularity.

Most everyone in the administration felt strongly about punishing the Russians—hard— after their 2016 interference. Trump had a different view. While he may not have colluded with Russia as a presidential candidate, at a minimum he cheered them on. "Russia, if you're listening," he bellowed at a campaign event in July 2016, "I hope you're able to find the thirty thousand [Clinton] emails that are missing. I think you will probably be rewarded mightily by the press." It was the first time in memory a US presidential candidate urged a foreign power to conduct espionage against his opponent. The same day, Russian hackers attempted to gain access to Secretary Clinton's personal office, and in the following weeks, Trump was gleeful at the turmoil caused by Moscow's ongoing leaks of other stolen emails.

After it became clear that the Kremlin was actively working to manipulate the election, Trump was nonetheless effusive in his praise for the dictator. "If he says great things about me, I'm going to say great things about him," the candidate confessed to reporters. "I've already said, he is really very much of a leader. I mean, you can say, oh, isn't that a terrible thing—the man has very strong control over a country…But certainly, in that system, he's been a leader, far more than our president has been a leader." He relished Putin's mockery of his defeated opponent after the election, tweeting: "Vladimir Putin said today about Hillary and Dems: 'In my opinion, it is humiliating. One must be able to lose with dignity.' So true!"

The president's denial-turned-apathy to Moscow's actions is why America responded with the diplomatic equivalent of a whimper to one of the biggest ever foreign affronts against our democracy. Of all the failures of Trump's foreign policy, letting Russia off the hook is perhaps the most frustrating. The outgoing Obama administration imposed modest sanctions on Moscow, including expelling several dozen alleged Russian agents from the United States, but it left the rest to the incoming White House. Trump was reluctant to take further action that might offend Putin, with whom he hoped to develop a close working relationship. He hesitated to even raise the subject in conversations with the Russian leader, dumbfounding people on the inside.

I remember when Congress sanctioned Russia in summer 2017. Representatives vented their anger over how little the administration had done to hold Russia accountable, so they took matters into their own hands and passed legislation punishing the country. Though he would later take credit for the sanctions to claim our administration had been unusually tough on Moscow, Trump in fact was furious. He felt Congress was getting in the way of his goal of a warm friendship with the Kremlin. Russia responded to the sanctions by kicking out hundreds of US embassy staff from their country and seizing US diplomatic compounds. President Trump's response was startling.

"I want to thank him because we're trying to cut down on payroll," Trump told reporters about Putin's move, without a hint of irony. "And as far as I'm concerned, I'm very thankful that he let go a large number of people, because now we have a smaller payroll. There's no real reason for them to go back. So I greatly appreciate the fact that we've been able to cut our payroll of the United States. We'll save a lot of money."

The president's obvious admiration for Vladimir Putin ("great guy," "terrific person") still continues to puzzle us, including those on the team who shrug off his outlandish behavior. Where did the Putin hero worship come from? It's almost as if Trump is the scrawny kid trying to suck up to the bully on the playground. Commentators have speculated, without any evidence, that Moscow must "have something" on the president. I wish I could say. All I know is that whatever drives his love for Putin, it's terrible for the United States because Vladimir is not on our side and no US president should be building him up.

We need a comprehensive strategy to counter the Russians, not court them. But Trump is living on another planet, one where he and Putin are companions and where Russia wants to help America be successful. As a result, US officials fear they're "on their own" in fighting back against Moscow. They're right. They are. If an agency wants to respond to Russia's anti-US behavior around the world, they shouldn't plan on steady air cover from the president. In fact, officials know they risk Trump's ire if the subject comes up in public interviews or congressional testimony. "I don't care," one fellow senior leader snapped when reminded by his staff that he needed to watch his words in Senate meetings. "He can fire me if he wants. I'm going to tell the truth. The Russians are not our friends."

Trump was once asked during a meeting with Putin whether he raised the subject of election interference. In response to the question, the president turned and offered a light-hearted scolding to his counterpart, wagging his finger. "Don't meddle in the election, please." Away from the cameras, advisors groaned. We were similarly confounded in Helsinki, when Trump insisted on having a private two-hour meeting with the Russian president, with no advisors present. This hardly ever happens. What is communicated between world leaders, especially competitors, can easily be misunderstood or misrepresented when there aren't witnesses to the conversation on both sides. Meeting with Putin privately was a risky move in light of allegations about collusion, and it remains a mystery to us why he demanded it.

I want to make a side note here. The president's secretive interactions with foreign leaders is generally concerning. International negotiations are often kept under wraps for good reason, but Trump's efforts have gone beyond the norm. When he hides them from members of his own administration, it should set off alarm bells. What arrangements does he make with regimes like Russia behind closed doors? Why doesn't he want people to know? The Ukraine scandal demonstrates that it's not beneath Trump to inappropriately ask personal favors of foreign leaders and submit more lamentable requests. Even if the Ukraine inquiry concludes Trump didn't commit a federal crime or the Republican Senate declines to convict him, voters should weigh these episodes seriously in the 2020 election. We should see Trump's actions as fireable offenses, regardless of whether or not Congress determines they are impeachable ones. If the president is reelected, you can count on the fact that he will make other dishonorable requests of foreign powers that Americans and his advisors are unlikely to know about. I, for one, don't want this president cutting secret deals with Vladimir Putin.

Trump's cavalier attitude toward the Russian security threat has had a predictable yet devastating consequence. Moscow has not been deterred from attacking American interests. It has been emboldened. They continue to take advantage of the United States, around the world and on our own soil. Former director of National Intelligence Dan Coats testified in January 2019 that Russia was still sowing social, racial, and political discord in the United States through influence operations, and several months later, Robert Mueller said the same. "It wasn't a single attempt," he testified to Congress. "They're doing it as we sit here. And they expect to do it during the next campaign."

This should be a national scandal, a cause for outrage and action against the Russian government. Instead, it's being ignored where it should matter most—in the Oval Office. Reporters asked Trump about Mueller's assessment days later and quizzed him again on whether he'd pressed Putin on the topic.

"You don't really believe this," he shot back. "Do you believe this? Okay, fine. We didn't talk about it." Then he boarded Marine One.

The person he *does* believe is Putin. According to a former top FBI official, Trump at one point rejected information he received regarding a rogue country's missile capability. He said the Russian president had given him different information, so it didn't matter what US spy agencies said. "I don't care. I believe Putin," the official quoted him as saying.

Willful ignorance is the fairest way to describe the president's attitude toward our enemies. He sees what he wants to see. If Trump likes a foreign leader, he refuses to accept the danger they might pose or ulterior motives they bring to the table. That's what makes it so easy for him to offhandedly dismiss detailed US threat assessments about nation-states or urgent alerts from our closest allies.

North Korea is another troubling example, one that may be odder than the president's infatuation with Russia.

Trump is fascinated by the country's young dictator, Kim Jong Un. "How many guys—he was like twenty-six or twenty-five when his father died—take over these tough generals, and all of a sudden...he goes in, he takes over, and he's the boss," he said in awe at an event when speaking about Kim's rise. "It's incredible. He wiped out the uncle, he wiped out this one, that one. I mean, this guy doesn't play games." Trump proposed meeting with the leader during the presidential race, a proposal that was rejected by North Korea as a propaganda ploy.

Once in the White House, the president went the other direction. He announced a policy of "maximum pressure" toward the north, punishing the regime for its aggressive behavior. Advisors traveled the world whipping up support for sanctions to further isolate Pyongyang. We were relieved, frankly, because we thought the president was taking a clear-eyed view of the situation, standing up against a horrible government that was not only producing nuclear weapons but starving and torturing its own people. It felt like a righteous cause, and we were proud to be getting tough in a place where other presidents had prostrated themselves.

But Trump couldn't hold the line for very long. He wanted badly to make a deal with Kim, whom he called "a pretty smart cookie," though top advisors warned him against it. Many administrations have been trapped in failed negotiations with North Korea, discussions that the regime exploited to buy time and build weapons. It was a bad idea to fall for it again unless circumstances changed dramatically.

Then one day Trump's unpredictability doctrine kicked in. South Korean officials were visiting

Washington to deliver a message that the north wanted to negotiate over its nuclear program. The president brought the officials into the Oval Office, where they reported that Kim wanted to meet personally. Trump, who months earlier had threatened North Korea with "fire and fury," agreed on the spot. Aides—including senior officials at the Departments of State and Defense—were caught off guard. Trump said he would speak to Kim face-to-face, the first meeting between an American president and his North Korean counterpart.

Externally, the White House billed the announcement as an exciting breakthrough. It offered the possibility of reducing tensions on the Korean Peninsula and created hope for a denuclearization deal. Internally, we thought it was very stupid. Only hours earlier, Secretary of State Rex Tillerson told reporters it was far too soon to think about negotiations between US and North Korean officials, let alone a meeting of the two countries' leaders. To put Trump and Kim in the same room, we thought, there would need to be major concessions from the North Koreans. Rex's view was that we weren't going to give them an audience with the most powerful man on earth without forcing them to pay a price; that is, until Trump decided otherwise.

"Maximum pressure" gave way to warm appease-ment. Almost immediately, the president was car-ried away with the theatrics over the substance. Planning began for a summit in Singapore like it was Trump's quinceañera. It would be a show to remember, proving he was a real grown-up states-man. Someone on cable news suggested Trump might get a Nobel Prize for making peace with Pyongyang, an idea that excited the president. The great dealmaker wanted to make a deal at almost any price, and Kim Jong Un, that smart cookie, knew it.

It was unclear to observers precisely how the United States would convince North Korea to give up its nuclear bombs when other administrations failed to do the same. The strategy and details didn't really matter to President Trump, though. He was so confident in his ability to forge a personal con-nection with Kim that it wasn't really about the details. It was about the chemistry. Unsurprisingly, the Singapore Summit flopped. It didn't produce any meaningful results, and aides felt validated in their view that chemistry was no substitute for hard diplomacy.

Trump was undeterred. He measured success differently. "I like him, he likes me," he said at a rally a few months after meeting Kim. "I guess that's okay. Am I allowed to say that?" He affectionately described the communications between the two leaders. "We went back and forth, then we fell in love. He wrote me beautiful letters, and they're great letters. We fell in love." In my time in public service, I never thought I would witness a grown man in the Oval Office fawn over a thuggish autocrat like an adoring teenage fan. Naive doesn't begin to describe it. Not a single member of the administration—not Rex Tillerson, not Jim Mattis, not Dan Coats, not Mike Pompeo, not Nikki Haley, not Mike Pence—would have spoken that way. Had anyone but Trump said something like that, they'd have been laughed out of the White House. It certainly seems they are laughing in North Korea.

With little progress being made on disarmament talks, our administration put more pressure on Pyongyang. This set the president off. In late 2018, the Treasury Department publicly sanctioned three regime officials for human rights abuses. Trump was furious. "Who did this?" he raged at advisors. "Kim is my friend!"

I lamented to another official that the president was losing sight of reality. North Korea's government was brutal, untrustworthy, and unlikely to compromise at the end of the day. She agreed, and soon after, Trump's intelligence chiefs echoed the warning in public testimony. North Korea was performing the same song and dance it always did to get the West off its back, offering a faux olive branch to relieve the pressure until a new US administration came into power.

As we tried to make sense of Donald Trump's positions or when one of us tried to argue against them, we first had to ask: Why is the president so attracted to autocrats? After a contentious meeting about the president's engagement with a foreign dictator, a top national security aide offered me his take. "The president sees in these guys what he wishes he had: total power, no term limits, enforced popularity, and the ability to silence critics for good." He was spot on. It was the simplest explanation.

For instance, Donald Trump sympathized with Saudi crown prince bin Salman's violent internal purge in 2017, saying the country's leaders "know exactly what they are doing" and adding that "some of those they are harshly treating have been 'milking' their country for years!" This included long-time US interlocutors who were allegedly held against their will, beaten, imprisoned, or put under house arrest.

He celebrated Chinese president Xi Jinping's move to permanently install himself in office for life, calling it an "extraordinary elevation," and telling him privately that he was a "king" for having made the bold move.

He enthused to reporters about Kim Jong Un's ability to control his population: "He's the head of a country, and I mean he's the strong head. Don't let anyone think anything different. He speaks, and his people sit up at attention. I want my people to do the same."

And he commiserated with Putin about the free press in the United States, telling the notorious thug, "You don't have this problem in Russia, but we do."

Trump's affinity for autocrats means we are flying blind through world affairs. The moral compass in the cockpit, the one that has charted America's course for decades, is broken. The president lacks a cogent agenda for dealing with these rivals because he doesn't recognize them as long-term threats. He only sees near-term deals. "Russia is a foe in certain respects. China is a foe economically...But that doesn't mean they are bad," the president said in one interview. "It doesn't mean anything. It means that they are competitive. They want to do well, and we want to do well." To him, adversaries are just trading partners to be haggled with until we get a fair shake, and once we do, it's a win for everyone.

What he doesn't see, especially with China, Russia, Iran, and North Korea, is that their governments are programmed to oppose us. They represent the opposite of our values. No "deal" will change that. Until their political systems shift fundamentally or they lose power, they will stand against the free and open international order America built. Like us, they will try to shape the world in their own image. Unlike us, their leaders don't care about natural rights and are gearing up for a protracted competition.

China should be our biggest worry. In his first-ever speech on the Senate floor, Mitt Romney compared Beijing to "the cook that kills the frog in a pot of boiling water, smiling and cajoling as it slowly turns up the military and economic heat." Mitt is right. The United States is taking its eye off the ball with China, and our national response has been ad hoc and indecisive under President Trump. We have no serious plan to safeguard our "empire of liberty" against China's rise. There is only the ever-changing negotiating positions of a grifter in chief, which will not be enough to win what is fast becoming the next Cold War.

President Trump is myopically focused on trade with China, which is only part of the picture. There are many other areas where aides agree we should be holding the Communist government's feet to the fire. Yet the foreign policy team can't really get him to focus on anything but the trade war. Americans should ask: Where is his Chinese human rights policy? Why is he so silent about the most significant pro-democracy demonstrations in the regime in two decades, when folks around him are pushing him to act? Where is his defense policy? Where is his proposal to contest China's influence region by region? Is there any long-term plan? There are government bureaucrats who care about these questions and have their own designs. We've discussed ideas around the table, but it doesn't matter if it isn't part of a bigger plan. The president can say he wants to keep his enemies guessing, but we all know those are the words of a man *without* a plan.

Our enemies and adversaries recognize the president is a simplistic pushover. They are unmoved by his bellicose Twitter threats because they know he can be played. President Trump is easily swayed by their rhetoric. We can all see it. He is visibly moved by flattery. He folds in negotiations, and he is willing to give up the farm for something that merely looks like a good deal, whether it is or not. They believe he is weak, and they take advantage of him. When they cannot, they simply ignore him.

Alienating Allies

The president's attraction to dictators would be less worrisome if it were matched by an equal affinity for our friends. The opposite is true. President Trump frequently alienates America's most important partners and personally disparages their leaders. His burn-the-house-down exit from the G7 summit in Canada—where he blasted Western friends while en route to meet an Eastern foe— was just one example of his inverted international priorities.

Recall that the president repudiated this type of behavior only months before taking office. "We've picked fights with our oldest friends," he warned, criticizing Obama's foreign policy. "And now they're starting to look elsewhere for help. Remember that. *Not good.*" Allies hoped President Trump would live up to these words, and some did admit to us they felt the Obama administration had given them the cold shoulder. We had an opportunity to win them back.

Hope didn't last. Right after the inauguration, President Trump made introductory phone calls to foreign heads of state. His conversation with Australian prime minister Malcolm Turnbull, a close US ally, was a sign of what was to come. The prime minister pressed the president on whether he would follow through with a deal on refugees previously negotiated between the two countries. "This deal will make me look terrible," he reportedly told Turnbull. "I think it is a horrible deal, a disgusting deal that I would have never made." Despite the prime minister's attempt to reason with him, Trump shut down the conversation. "I have had it. I have been making these calls all day, and this is the most unpleasant call all day." Then he hung up.

Summaries of presidential phone calls with foreign leaders are typically written up afterward and distributed within the White House and to other officials with the appropriate clearances. This is standard practice. The transcripts help a president's lieutenants to stay in sync with their boss when engaging the same countries. After details leaked from Trump's early calls, the summaries were put on lockdown. The distribution was limited mostly for security reasons, but also because the content was so routinely and so remarkably embarrassing.

No major US ally has been spared from the

president's indignities. In private, he pillories partner nations and their leaders and is not shy about doing the same in the open, as in the case of his comment about the Canadian prime minister being "very dishonest & weak," only hours after being hosted by the northern neighbor. He's done the same with France, mocking President Emmanuel Macron on Twitter for his low approval ratings and high unemployment, and with Germany, criticizing Chancellor Angela Merkel's administration for failing to reduce crime and accusing its leaders of being freeloaders that take advantage of US generosity.

The United Kingdom, with which the United States has a "special relationship," is no exception. After multiple terrorist attacks rocked Britain in 2017, the president scolded the Brits for failing to rein in extremism. "Another attack in London by a loser terrorist," he tweeted after a train bombing in September 2017. "These are sick and demented people who were in the sights of Scotland Yard. Must be proactive!" Prime Minister Theresa May bristled at the accusation, telling reporters, "I never think it's helpful for anybody to speculate about what is an ongoing investigation." In the months to come, her team would become infuriated with our administration, as President Trump criticized

May's handling of Britain's exit from the European Union.

When confidential internal messages leaked detailing the British ambassador's critiques of the Trump administration (including the apt observations that the president is "unpredictable" and his White House "dysfunctional") the president proceeded to validate all of the ambassador's concerns with an intemperate overreaction. Rather than showing restraint, he punched down, tweeting that the ambassador was "a very stupid guy," "wacky," and a "pompous fool." For no strategic purpose, other than spitefulness, he also took parting shots at May, who was then stepping down as prime minister, calling her policies a disaster. "What a mess she and her representatives have created," the president said in July 2019, specifically honing in on Brexit. "I have told her how it should be done, but she decided to go another way…The good news for the wonderful United Kingdom is that they will soon have a new Prime Minister."

We have effectively given up on trying to block the president's criticisms of our friends. It can't be helped. He wants to say whatever he wants to say, as he does on any other issue. If anything, when he's told not to say something—to avoid criticizing a leader directly, for instance, or to keep himself from breaking a promise we've made—Trump will say it *louder*. After these outbursts, it's embarrassing for Trump lieutenants who need to ask the same foreign partners for help on something, whether it is to catch a wanted criminal or to support the United States in an important vote at the United Nations. Imagine someone announced to a crowd that you were a "pompous fool" and then rang you up for a favor. That's the sort of cool reception American officials receive all the time in foreign meetings.

President Trump does more than humiliate America's friends. He takes actions or threatens to take actions that will damage them in the long run. For example, Trump has hit Western partners with trade penalties, invoking "national security" provisions of US law to counter what he says are unfair economic practices in places such as Europe. He was on the brink of pulling out of a trade deal with South Korea in the midst of tense discussions on North Korea, putting the US ally in an awkward position. He threatened to scrap a longstanding US defense treaty with Japan, speculating that if America was attacked, the Japanese would not come to our aid but would instead "watch it on a Sony television." And he regularly threatens to discard existing or pending international agreements with our friends in order to get them to do what he wants, including displaying personal fealty toward him.

You can't overstate how damaging these presidential whims are to US security. Has it caused us to take a major credibility hit overseas? You bet. We see it all the time. Our closest partners are more guarded toward us than ever before, and it causes dissension within our own team. Every time he back-hands an ally, top officials complain it's not worth bringing up foreign policy developments anymore with the president, for fear that he'll kick over the LEGO structures diplomats have patiently built alongside our partners. "There's no way I'm raising that in the Oval Office with him," someone might say. "You know it will set him off." This isn't helpful either. The president shouldn't be kept in the dark, yet people worry informing him will cause more harm than good. Others have just decided to resign, unwilling to be party to the dissolution of America's alliances.

President Trump has repeatedly astounded advisors by saying he wants to exit our biggest alliance of them all: the North Atlantic Treaty Organization (NATO). This would be a huge gift to the Russians, who have long opposed the twenty-nine-nation group. NATO has been the backbone of international security for more than a half century, but the president tells us we are "getting raped" because other countries are spending far less than the United States to be a part of it, adding that the organization is "obsolete." The president is correct that a number of nations aren't spending enough on defense and that America has carried the over-whelming military burden. But the United States is also the most powerful nation on earth, and the investments we make in the NATO alliance allow us to project our influence globally to stop danger before it comes our way. Leaving the alliance would not only be foolish but suicidal—an advertisement to foreign enemies that it's open season against Western countries, each left to fend for themselves.

His ultimatums were unacceptable to some cabinet officials. Rex Tillerson and Jim Mattis, for example, specifically adjusted their travel plans to reassure America's allies of our commitments, despite counterproductive Trump statements to the contrary. Some might say this came close to insubordination. It didn't. It would have been der-eliction of duty to sit by and let our security part-nerships wither, and I find it hard to imagine that Trump supporters, who tend to be staunch backers of the military, would be pleased if the president pulled America out of the most powerful military compact in world history. They should be grateful there are folks who've talked him down and who've kept a reassuring hand on the backs of our allies.

A handful of America's clever partners have decided they don't want to wait around to get attacked and ostracized by the president. They've learned how to play him to maintain good relations and shift the partnership to their advantage. Our Israeli friends have watched dictators lavish Trump with praise and have learned to similarly cater to his self-conceit in order to get what they want. They've named settlements after him and found other extravagant ways to tell Trump how great he is, habitually exploiting the president's pride to exact concessions. I probably don't need to say it, but we don't want this to become the norm either.

I suppose some Americans don't care about foreign policy until a threat reaches our shores. They should care, because the actions we take abroad—or don't take—determine whether the United States is safe in the long run. Our friends are among the best stockades against foreign hostility. We're talking about countries that come to our aid when disaster strikes; that stand up for us in contentious international disputes; that protect our ships, planes, and people; and that are willing to fight and die alongside our troops in remote deserts. They are not, as Trump will tell anyone who cares to listen, out to screw us. *We need them.* Will Durant argued that the laws of nature—including "the survival of the fittest"—apply to global politics. In nature, cooperation is one of the keys to winning any competition. We cooperate within our families, our communities, and societies in order to overcome threats. We must do the same on the world stage, sticking close to our allies so the United States not only survives, but thrives.

But they no longer trust us. Why should they? Like anyone else, they can't predict the president's erratic behavior, and they find his attitude toward them demeaning. I know he lies to their faces (or on the phone) by offering false assurance of his support. He exposes sensitive discussions we have with them, and he tries to bully them into submission. Consequently, many are planning for life without the United States or, worse, how to deal with us as a competitor. The president of the European Council tweeted a viewpoint shared by many of his colleagues in May 2018, writing, "Looking at the latest decisions of @realDonaldTrump someone could even think: with friends like that who needs enemies."

President Trump's overall alienation of our

closest partners is putting the United States at risk. Historically, our partnerships have given us an advantage over other countries. Our enemies have few friends, while America has many. We can't afford a change in that calculus.

The Choice

The world depends on the United States to shape history. No person recognized this fact better than Winston Churchill, whose nation depended on American intervention in the Second World War. At the time, he wrote, "How heavily do the destinies of this generation hang upon the government and people of the United States...Will the United States throw their weight into the scales of peace and law and freedom while time remains, or will they remain spectators until the disaster has occurred; and then, with infinite cost and labor, build up what need not have been cast down?"

Are we still willing to throw our weight onto the scales of freedom? Will we be spectators? Or has President Trump decided we are on the wrong team—that we should be in a small club of thugs or a big club of free nations?

The world isn't sure which way we'll go. Surveys

reveal America's international image has plummeted under President Trump and that respondents believe the United States is failing to step up to solve international challenges. According to the Pew Research Center, "favorable" views of the United States are at record lows in many nations, and more countries say relations with Washington have worsened, not improved, during Trump's tenure.

The reputational free fall stems from confusion the president has created with his words and actions. Under his leadership, it appears the United States is switching sides in global politics. In a July 2018 interview, the president was asked to name America's biggest global adversary. He didn't lead the list with China, which is stealing American innovation at a scale never before seen in history, or Russia, which is working to tear our country apart. He led off with a longtime ally. "Well, I think we have a lot of foes," he told the reporter. "I think the European Union is a foe—what they do to us in trade. Now, you wouldn't think of the European Union, but they're a foe."

Today the future of democracy is uncertain. Other nations are threatening our place atop the international order, and while it's not automatically bad for us to have peers, it *is* bad if they threaten our way of life. To guard against their nefarious designs, we must stick together and keep fighting for what we believe. We cannot rely on hope. Hope will not stop Iranian missiles or thwart Chinese espionage. As Kissinger wrote, the "goals of America's past—peace, stability, progress, and freedom for mankind—will have to be sought in a journey that has no end. 'Traveler,' says a Spanish proverb, 'there are no roads. Roads are made by walking.'"

Americans must decide which way we'll walk. If we want to prevail against aggressors, we must be ready for constant competition. We must be unhesitant in choosing between right and wrong. We must be very clear—our *leaders* must be very clear—about who is a friend and who is a foe. On that account, President Trump has failed us.

CHAPTER 6

The New Mason-Dixon Line

"If we are to have another contest in the near future of our national existence, I predict that the dividing line will not be Mason and Dixon's, but between patriotism and intelligence on the one side, and superstition, ambition, and ignorance on the other."
—*Ulysses S. Grant*

When constructing the American republic, the history of Ancient Greece weighed heavily on the minds of the Founding Fathers and is relevant for understanding the implications of the Trump presidency. You see, Athens was the cautionary tale of how self-government could go wrong. It was an example of "direct democracy," a society where the majority ruled and where citizens participated personally in the assembly, voting on the issues of the day by raising their hands. At first this was revolutionary, but in time, a herd-like mentality overcame the system. In the heat of the moment, the passions of the people could turn them into an angry mob, leading the majority into destructive decisions that proved to be their undoing.

The Greek experiment with democracy reached a memorable turning point in 427 BC. Athens was at war and tensions were high. The decisions the Athenian people faced were not mundane matters of bureaucracy, but life and death. Debates in the assembly were contentious, and powerful orators stirred up public anxiety. That year one of their long-standing allies—a city-state called Mytilene—defected and joined Athens's enemy Sparta. The Athenians quashed the revolt, but they feared that if they didn't punish the Mytilenians, other allies might abandon them, too. So the Athenian Assembly voted to kill all the city's men and enslave its women and children to prove a point. The next day, citizens got cold feet and called for another meeting to reconsider the hasty decision.

One of the most vocal speakers in the debate was Cleon. He will sound familiar to readers. A prominent Athenian, Cleon inherited money from his father and leveraged it to launch a career in politics. Historians have characterized him as a populist, one of the era's "new politicians." Cleon was a crass and blunt public speaker, an immoral man who frequently sued his opponents, an armchair critic of those in power, and an orator who preyed upon the emotions of the people to whip up public support for his opinions. Although some accounts characterize him as charming, his speaking style was said to be angry and repugnant. Aristotle later described Cleon as: "[T]he man who, with his attacks, corrupted the Athenians more than anyone else. Although other speakers behaved decently, Cleon was the first to shout during a speech in the Assembly, [and] use abusive language while addressing the people...."

Cleon argued for slaughtering the Mytilenian rebels. He disparaged the "foolish" public intellectuals opposed to the decision and urged Athenians to ignore them. The educated politicians couldn't be trusted; he suggested they might have been "bribed" to mislead the public. Government was best left to plain-speaking "ordinary men," like himself. Cleon argued that no one had ever hurt their empire as much as Mytilenians, whose defection was an "attempt to ruin us." He warned that if they didn't make an example of the rebels, Athens would waste more money in more foreign wars, fighting people who defied them. Cleon closed by telling the assembly not to be "traitors to yourselves," to show no "mercy" or "pity," to listen to their original gut instincts, and to "punish them as they deserve."

A man named Diodotus responded. He argued that ill-tempered decisions were reckless. Deliberation was necessary before taking action. Anyone who argued otherwise was either "senseless" or was trying to scare the people with false statements, such as Cleon's insinuation that the other side in the debate had been bribed. "The good citizen ought to triumph not by frightening his opponents but by beating them fairly in argument," Diodotus shot back. He said mass slaughter would be contrary to Athens's long-term interests and that being lenient would instead allow Athens to win over many Mytilenians whom they still needed as supporters.

The assembly took it to a vote: Kill and enslave the Mytilenians, or show mercy by holding only the rebel leaders accountable? There was no consensus. With a show of hands, Athenians were almost evenly split. According to historical accounts, when the counting was completed, Diodotus secured just enough supporters to carry the day. With that, a horrific atrocity was prevented.

The story doesn't have a happy ending. The split vote demonstrated how persuasive Cleon's rhetoric had been, flashing the dark underbelly of majority rule. It was a preview of Athens's descent. Within a decade, Athenians faced a similar decision. This time, they chose to throw mercy to the wind and annihilated the island people of Melos. Within three decades, a mob assembly voted to put to death Socrates, the so-called "wisest man" to have ever lived. The latter was an exclamation point on the death of Athenian democracy, which never recovered its former glory and eventually slipped into tyranny.

Like Athens, we face a turning point. The tone of our national conversation has taken a nosedive. We've grown impatient with our bureaucracies, with our Congress, and with one another. We've retreated into ideological corners. At the same time, the decisions we face are not routine; they are of the highest consequence, from an exploding federal debt to protracted foreign conflicts. Resolving them requires us to come together to set the nation's priorities through conversation and compromise. Yet we are more divided than ever. The foundations of our democracy, which were meant to set boundaries on majority rule, are being tested.

Like Athens, we also have a Cleon in our midst, a foul-mouthed populist politician who uses rhetoric as a loaded gun. I'm not the first to see the similarities. Donald Trump's words are powerful, and we are suffering three primary consequences from them. First, his words are hardening the national discourse, making it more difficult to sustain civility. Second, they are undermining our perceptions of the truth, making it challenging to find common ground. And third, they are fanning the flames of the mob mentality our Founders tried to prevent, making reasonable people once again consider—and lament—democracy's greatest weakness.

Nasty Man

The words of America's chief executives are captured after every administration, bound into volumes known as Public Papers of the Presidents. The compilations become the official record of each leader's writings and speeches, published after they leave office. When I walk into the West Wing of the White House, the Papers are one of the first sights that catch my eye, displayed inside an ornate bookcase directly inside the official entrance. The volumes contain the words that shaped our nation and shook the world, reverberating through history.

Flipping through the pages, readers might encounter President Lincoln's stirring remarks, which steered the United States toward reconciliation after a bitter Civil War. "With malice toward none, with charity for all, with firmness in the right as God gives us to see the right, let us strive on to finish the work we are in, to bind up the nation's wounds, to care for him who shall have borne the battle and for his widow and his orphan, to do all which may achieve and cherish a just and lasting peace among ourselves and with all nations." They might find Franklin Delano Roosevelt's speech after the surprise attack at Pearl Harbor. "No matter how long it may take us to overcome this premeditated invasion, the American people in their righteous might will win through to absolute victory...We will not only defend ourselves to the uttermost, but will make very certain that this form of treachery shall never again endanger us."

What will the future volumes of President Trump's Public Papers tell us about him and this moment in our political life? Will they inspire us and record a new birth of unity in our country? Or will we read them years from now as if they were the Mytilenian Debate, words that marked a turning point toward greater division?

A Warning

We don't know yet how his Public Papers will end, but we certainly know how they will begin. They will open with his inaugural address, which was characteristic of President Trump's coarse style. That day he painted a bleak view of the country, of "mothers and children trapped in poverty in our inner cities; rusted-out factories scattered like tombstones across the landscape of our nation; an education system, flush with cash but that leaves our young and beautiful students deprived of knowledge; and the crime and gangs and drugs that have stolen too many lives and robbed our country of so much unrealized potential." He said our money had been "ripped" from our homes and "redistributed" around the world, while countries were ravaging us by "stealing our companies and destroying our jobs."

It was a scene of "American carnage," Trump explained. With him in charge, we would "start winning again, winning like never before." We would be "unstoppable." His presidency would make us "strong," "wealthy," "proud," and "safe" again. The carnage would end. Those of us watching the event on the West Front of the US Capitol Building were perplexed. This was a moment to unite and inspire. But his remarks were resentful and foreboding. Looking back, I find it oddly fitting that the very moment he started speaking it began to rain.

Ironically, his grim portrayal of America will be among the more eloquent statements in President Trump's Public Papers because he read what he was handed. As we know, he usually speaks less cogently. He meanders off script, focusing on a main idea only in fits and starts, and revels in distractions, especially broadsides against his critics. This is a constant annoyance for aides who spend time crafting speeches so his words are more artful and less offensive. He often scraps those prepared remarks on the spot, allowing us to hear from the real Donald Trump—a man whose natural oratory is crude and mean spirited.

Why does this matter? Because words matter. As a student of history, I've always believed a president's words are especially important because he (and one day, she) speaks for all of us. They shape how we engage with one another and how we meet the country's needs. They influence the way we address challenges and how we cooperate within the same government. A leader's words become the rallying cries for our shared causes, from what we stand against ("No taxation without representation!") to what we stand for ("We choose to go to the moon in this decade!"). Unfortunately,

Trump's words don't foster national civility. They corrode it.

His words sound more like those of a two-bit bartender at a rundown barrelhouse than a president. At any given event, Trump might praise someone who assaulted a journalist: "Any guy that can do a body slam, he's my kind of—he's my guy." He might lambast his opponents as "low testosterone" or "low IQ." Or he might mock a sexual-assault accuser's testimony, mimicking her voice and the lawyer questioning her: "*I had one beer. How did you get home? I don't remember. How'd you get there? I don't remember. Where is the place? I don't remember. How many years ago was it? I don't know. I don't know. I don't know. I don't know...But I had one beer. That's the only thing I remember.*" He writes off her accusation as false.

Most notably, President Trump's Papers will be filled with the pugilistic social media commentary that has dominated our public conversations. Future historians will need only to throw a dart at the calendar to find the vitriol. Let's say April 1, 2018. That week his Papers will record that the president blasted ABC News, CBS, CNN, MSNBC, NBC, and the *Washington Post* (all individually) as "fake news"; blamed online retailer Amazon for stores closing "all over the country"; ridiculed the "money-losing" US Postal Service; mocked former US trade negotiators as "foolish, or incompetent"; denounced Mexico on immigration and threatened to cut off their "cash cow, NAFTA"; lamented his own Justice Department and FBI as "an embarrassment to our country"; and rounded it off by deriding his predecessor as "Cheatin' Obama."

That "April Fools" week was not special for any reason. It was like every week. The overall volume of the president's sensationalist rhetoric is astounding, and it will all be archived for posterity, showing Donald Trump to be the least articulate president of all time. It's not just that his style of communicating is rambling or contentious. It's that he's laid waste to public decency. During the presidential debates, Trump told us not to elect Hillary Clinton—"Such a nasty woman," he said of her. Well, he got it his way, and instead we ended up with a nasty man.

Not a single day goes by that President Trump's outrageous statements don't confound someone on his team, if not all of us. I know other administrations dealt with this every once in a while. Obama's cabinet officials complained quietly that their boss would talk an issue to death and couldn't make up his mind. Bush aides winced at the president's foot-in-mouth moments. However, I also know that none of them had to deal with these frustrations on a daily basis.

Past presidential appointees didn't have to wake up each morning to discover, in a full-blown panic, that the president woke up before them and was making wild and vulgar pronouncements to the world. When you bump into former officials in the course of Washington business, they ask what it's like to operate in this type of environment. I'll tell you. It's like showing up at the nursing home at daybreak to find your elderly uncle running pantsless across the courtyard and cursing loudly about the cafeteria food, as worried attendants try to catch him. You're stunned, amused, and embarrassed all at the same time. Only your uncle probably wouldn't do it *every single day*, his words aren't broadcast to the public, and he doesn't have to lead the US government once he puts his pants on.

Donald Trump's words do more than drive his team crazy. They are dividing Americans. He may start fights on Twitter and at the microphones, but we are continuing them at home. Political differences between Americans are now at record highs. Studies show that Republicans are becoming more partisan, unwilling to veer from the party line, and Democrats are doing the same. The one thing the two sides *can* agree on is that the phenomenon is real. A Pew Research Center survey released in 2019 found that a whopping 85 percent of US adults said that "political debate in the country has become more negative and less respectful," and two-thirds said it is less focused on the issues. Where do they pin the blame? A majority believed President Trump "has changed the tone and nature of political debate for the worse."

The verbal acrimony has real-world consequences. Our divisions make us less likely to engage with one another, less likely to trust our government, and less optimistic about our country's future. When asked to look outward to the year 2050, Americans were deeply pessimistic, according to another survey. A majority of respondents predicted the United States would be in decline, burdened by economic disparity and more politically polarized. Nearly the same percentage of Democrats and Republicans agreed on the last point.

In the nation's capital, the president's bull-in-a-china-shop language is inhibiting his own agenda. He can't get consensus on Capitol Hill, even on previously uncontroversial issues, because his style has alienated potential partners on both sides. Democrats aren't exactly trying to restore bipartisanship, but there might be more hope if the figurehead of the Republican Party were not treating them as mortal enemies rather than political opponents. Instead, every big idea becomes radioactive upon release. Every line of the budget is a trench on the political battlefield. We constantly struggle to sell the president's priorities because he is his own worst enemy. Just when it seems like there is a breakthrough behind the scenes on a tough issue, the president might blow it up by verbally assailing the person we're negotiating with or changing his position.

For instance, there was the time we'd painstakingly sketched the broad outlines of a nearly $2 trillion agreement with the Democrats to repair America's aging infrastructure. Fixing America's roads and bridges is a popular, bipartisan policy and could have been a slam dunk for Donald Trump, who is an actual builder and understands the issue. Many of us in the administration cared about it. Trump claimed he did, too. Then the president, angry at what he'd seen on cable news, walked into a White House meeting with House Speaker Nancy Pelosi and Senate Majority Leader Chuck Schumer, threw away his talking points, and said he couldn't work with them until they stopped investigating his administration. They didn't get a word in edgewise. He stormed out to the Rose Garden after a few minutes and angrily told reporters that Democrats couldn't "investigate and legislate simultaneously" and that they needed to "get these phony investigations over with" before he'd talk. Prospects for an infrastructure pact vanished in an instant. Next time you're stuck in traffic or on a pothole-ridden federal highway, remember this episode.

The inability to bite his tongue is the second-worst trait any president can have when he's trying to make deals on behalf of the American people. The worst is dishonesty.

Big Little Lies

Fact-checking is an important function in any White House. Before draft remarks ever hit the paper, ideas are discussed in staff meetings and vetted. Perhaps it's a speech about space travel. A data call goes out to different offices and agencies looking for facts to build around a core narrative. Then a speechwriter takes a first pass. It gets farmed out to policy experts to make sure it's consistent with administration policy. A second draft is made before it's passed to an internal fact-checker to independently confirm each detail. Then aides read it again, including maybe the chief of staff, before it goes to the president or vice president for final review.

This is what happened in March 2019 when Vice President Mike Pence made a rousing speech about the US space program in Huntsville, Alabama. NASA helped supply the facts in order to craft a big announcement. "At the direction of the president of the United States," Pence declared, "it is the stated policy of this administration to return American astronauts to the moon within the next five years. The first woman and the next man on the moon will both be American astronauts, launched by American rockets, from American soil!" The crowd was ecstatic.

You know what happened next. It's the twist in every Trump story that we all hope never comes but always does. The president stepped in, made a statement that no one fact-checked beforehand, and screwed it up. A few weeks after the Pence speech, Trump tweeted, "For all of the money we are spending, NASA should NOT be talking about going to the Moon - We did that 50 years ago. They should be focused on the much bigger things we are doing, including Mars (of which the Moon is a part), Defense and Science!" First, the tweet was misleading. The president himself had approved NASA's lunar plans; he was acting as if he hadn't. Some of us speculated it was because the moon wasn't big enough for him. Second, he made the very scientifically inaccurate claim that the moon is a part of Mars, despite being separated by nearly fifty million miles. Pence's staff, a bit befuddled, flagged the tweet internally to ensure someone corrected Trump. "There's no need to go to Mars," one aide messaged. "We're already on it!"

Earlier, we touched briefly upon President Trump's tenuous relationship with the truth. He makes outlandish claims, is drawn to conspiracy theories, and regularly spreads half-truths and demonstrably false information. That was not news to anyone when he joined the presidential race. Trump has been prone to misstatements for as long as he's been in the public eye. His family members laugh it off as harmless. Everyone knows it's his "style," they say, so what's the big deal? When it's bad facts about the solar system, they're right. It's harmless and even comical, but it's worse when it's a disproven claim that "millions" of people voted illegally in a national election.

The problem is that people believe what he says because he's the president, and Trump regularly—

frequently—spreads false information that large majorities of the country accept as the truth. I will be the first to say that political opponents have clouded our ability to judge the president's statements fairly because they have a knee-jerk reaction to *everything* he says. To them, it's all a lie. That's not accurate. *Everything* the president says is not a lie, but an awful lot of it is.

A *Washington Post* analysis found that after nearly nine hundred days in the White House, the president made a staggering eleven thousand junk claims. This averages out to more than ten half-truths or untruths a day. While some Americans have grown skeptical of a media that seems to attack President Trump relentlessly, this figure is based on objective analysis of his own words, words that can be proven inaccurate or flat-out wrong.

You can randomly search the databases of his claims and find everything from easily dismissed white lies ("I'm running the best economy in our history") to obvious whoppers ("I won the popular vote"). The president has repeatedly claimed he got NATO countries to spend $100 billion more on the alliance's defense. This is false. Countries were increasing their defense expenditures before Trump took office, and the increases are less than half of his claim. The president also said violent crime was surging in the two years before he took office—with murders up "by more than 20 percent"—and that he's brought crime down, even though two years before he was inaugurated the violent crime rate was at one of its lowest points in forty-five years. The list goes on and on.

The president's falsehoods are especially problematic when they change public attitudes. Misstating defense budgets and crime statistics is one thing. Every president slips up. But convincing the masses to share the absurd views we've discussed—that his opponents are actual criminals, that the FBI is corrupt, and that the judicial system is rigged—is far more consequential, with real-world social implications. You, the reader, might be more enlightened and dismiss these statements when you hear them, yet millions of people accept them as fact, changing the way they engage in politics.

The president has been called a pathological liar. I used to cringe when I heard people say that just to score political points, and I thought it was unfair. Now I know it's true. He spreads lies he hears. He makes up new lies to spread. He lies to our faces. He asks people around him to lie. People who've known him for years accept it as common knowledge. We cannot get used to this. Think of what we must "trust" a president to do as our chief executive. That's why we spent the beginning of this book assessing character, because it is so critical for our commander in chief to have it.

His appointees have the humiliating chore of defending him when he's wrong. If he says something false, he asks us to spin it closer to the truth. Advisors try to avoid admitting Trump was "wrong," and hilariously, this creates a second round of misleading statements, as aides create new lies about the president's old lies in order to bring them more in line with the facts. The ripple effect of excuses actually distorts reality. Because it's too confusing to follow, it's easier for people to either accept what the president said in the first place, or not. In the meantime, the truth lies unconscious and bleeding in a ditch along the side of the road.

President Trump is fundamentally undermining our perceptions of "truth." He has taken us down a dark, subjectivist rabbit hole. To him, there is no real truth. If people *believe* something is true, *that makes it true*. A scientist will tell you a tree is a tree. It cannot be both a tree and a sheep at the same time. Not for the president. A tree is only a tree to him if we all agree it is. If he can convince us it's a sheep, then it *is* a sheep!

Kellyanne Conway unintentionally summed up this Trumpian philosophy beautifully. She went on *Meet the Press* and was forced to defend the president's absurd boast about having the largest ever crowd at his inauguration. To be clear, the president's claim was easily disproven by facts and photographs and numbers and recorded history and basic human reasoning. Still, Chuck Todd pressed Conway on the subject, to which she responded: "You're saying it's a falsehood... [but] Sean Spicer, our press secretary, gave alternative facts."

"Wait a minute," Todd interjected. "Alternative facts?...Alternative facts are not facts. They're falsehoods."

She chided the host: "Your job is not to call things ridiculous that are said by our press secretary and our president. That is not your job."

In other words: *We said it, so it's true.*

Kellyanne is not a dumb person. She's smart, well-read, and normally quite considerate, but like everyone who hangs around Donald Trump too long, she's been forced to become a reality contortionist. This is what he asks of her, of anyone, to stay in his good graces. He enjoys watching people go out and compromise their integrity in order to serve him.

The president's untruths resonate with supporters due to their "confirmation bias." Humans tend to interpret new information as evidence to support preexisting views. For example, if you think dogs are dangerous and someone tells you that a rabid canine is roaming the neighborhood, you are more likely to accept it as a fact and less likely to question it as a rumor, because you already believe dogs are vicious. The social media age has put this cognitive defect on steroids. We can now reinforce our opinions instantly with supporting "facts" found in tweets, on blogs, on liberal or conservative websites, and beyond.

Donald Trump exacerbates this phenomenon by pandering to common prejudices with false information. When he does, the "false" part gets ignored by followers because of their confirmation bias. The "information" part gets absorbed. They are willing to march with him in lockstep if what he says validates what they already believe. This happens on both ends of the political spectrum, but the president exploits it to a level heretofore unseen. You think your government is corrupt? Donald Trump agrees with you, peddling conspiracies about a faceless Deep State secretly pulling the levers of government. Worried about illegal immigrants stealing US jobs by the millions? You should, he says, because they're swarming America and will probably be cleaning out your desk on Monday.

The epistemological crisis means Americans can't find common ground because they can't agree on the same set of facts. The president fudges the truth so frequently on so many issues that we have difficulty reaching a common starting point when we debate one another. Consequently, Americans can't move from the *what* to the *so what*—from the *facts* of a problem to a course of action for how to *solve* a problem. Even the little lies President Trump tells, when repeated over and over, have a big impact by gradually changing public perceptions of what is true and what matters.

We are now living in different realities. As evidence, a 2019 survey found Republicans and Democrats are further apart than ever on the issues they say should be the government's top priorities. The most recent study found "there is virtually no common ground in the priorities that rise to the top of the lists" between the two sides. Democratic respondents said our nation's biggest challenges were health care, education, the environment, Medicare, and poverty. Republicans said they were terrorism, the economy, Social

Security, immigration, and the military. It's the least amount of crossover the Pew Research Center has found since it began tracking these metrics more than two decades ago. Trump's rhetoric reinforces these divisions.

The president's unconcern about the truth has terrible implications for a free society. The Book of John says, "Ye shall know the truth, and the truth shall make you free." Our capacity to reason—to see through falsehoods—is one of our sturdiest ramparts against threats to democracy. Without it, our republic is vulnerable to creeping encroachments of authoritarianism. Trump's words have already undercut the independence of the judiciary, excused the overreach of executive power, and chipped away at public trust in government. They are also being used to attack our last hope for truth: the free press.

The president is engaged in an all-out, guns-a-blazing rhetorical battle against journalists. I know there are many Trump partisans who have no problem with the media getting its comeuppance for long-simmering bias against the GOP. That's the feeling inside the Trump administration, too. The communications team is gleeful when the president lobs a grenade at the press, yet the media, for all of its flaws, exists for a reason in a democracy. They are our defense against the government, a source of power that can't be censored. But since he can't censor them, President Trump has tried to do the next best thing and discredit them.

Trump has attacked the media on Twitter well over a thousand times since taking office and tweeted the phrase "fake news" five hundred plus times. His definition of "fake news" has evolved from outlets that report inaccurate information to outlets that criticize him. Privately and publicly, Trump has fumed at his coverage and looked for ways to retaliate against the news media, ranging from taking away access privileges for White House reporters to suggesting the government should open federal investigations into their reporting.

Trump's views on freedom of speech are most charitably described as perverted. He once said, "See, I don't think that the mainstream media is free speech either because it's so crooked. It's so dishonest. So to me, free speech is not when you see something good and then you purposely write bad. To me, that's very dangerous speech, and you become angry at it. But that's not free speech." That, of course, is the very definition of free speech—being able to criticize a president when he doesn't like it.

His attitude has trickled down to staff. I remember a rambling ninety-minute press conference in fall 2018 when the president got into it with CNN's Jim Acosta, who started asking uncomfortable questions about Russia. The president told him to sit down and called him a "rude, terrible person." Later in the day, Bill Shine, one of the many White House communications chiefs we've had, sauntered into a meeting. "Guess what I just did," he baited aides. "What?" they asked. "I blocked Acosta from getting into the White House. He's supposed to be on TV tonight from here, but he's about to find out that Secret Service won't let him in!" The team laughed and gave him high fives. Acosta could be a jerk sometimes, but I don't remember the part of civics class where being a jerk was a limitation on the freedom of the press.

Eventually the president adopted a more incendiary view of the media, "the enemy of the people," a term routinely used by the Soviet Union when imprisoning or torturing journalists who told the truth about the totalitarian state. After Trump first used the phrase, the United States Senate unanimously (as in every Democrat and Republican in the chamber) passed a resolution rebuking it. "Resolved, that the Senate affirms that the press is not the enemy of the people," it read, "reaffirms the vital and indispensable role the free press serves," and "condemns the attacks on the institution of the free press and views efforts to systematically undermine the credibility of the press as an attack on the democratic institutions of the United States."

Donald Trump's media hate is infectious. By the spring of 2018 more than half of all Republican voters polled said they agreed with the president that the media was the enemy of the people, while only 37 percent believed the free press was "an important part of democracy." These attitudes will have long-term repercussions on our ability to return to truth, perhaps even violent ones. A few months following the aforementioned poll, pipe bombs were sent to thirteen media outlets and personalities. All of them were figures President Trump had attacked by name, a chilling example of how his words can jump the tracks from careless rhetoric to real-world danger.

Pixelated Pitchforks

One of the Founders' deepest fears was the public mob mentality. That's why the direct democracy of

Athens became the opposite of what it was supposed to be. "Mob-rule is a rough sea for the ship of state to ride," an American historian once wrote. "Every wind of oratory stirs up the waters and deflects the course. The upshot of such a democracy is tyranny or autocracy; the crowd so loves flattery, it is so 'hungry for honey,' that at last the wiliest and most unscrupulous flatterer, calling himself the 'protector of the people,' rises to supreme power." That's when self-government implodes. The Founders set out to remedy this. They created representative government instead of direct democracy, staggered elections every few years to avoid the momentary impulses of the masses, and counted on the country's large size to make it hard for the demands of angry factions to spread from state to state.

The modern age is threatening our system in ways they could never have imagined. Representative government no longer insulates elected leaders from the sudden convulsions of the people. Today, members of Congress are harassed around the clock online. With every word and vote scrutinized, they are shying away from cooperation and adopting the tone of those who pressure them. Social media has allowed factions to form suddenly, cross boundaries virtually, and snowball, despite the large size of our nation. There is no longer any need for compromise when you can silence the opposition with virtual intimidation.

Our current president exploits the mob mentality, which is the most consequential aspect of his charged rhetoric.

Trump revels in the herd-like behavior of his followers. He uses his social media presence to inflame public debates and to dispatch supporters to attack politicians who've criticized him—or to rally followers in his defense. We all know that people are dumber and crueler in large groups. Trump plays this to his advantage by directing the violent energy toward whatever careless end he wishes. When the pixelated pitchforks get raised, truth becomes the first victim. Irrationality takes over. That's how the president turns his own fake news into instantaneous reality. His falsehoods get retweeted by the tens of thousands before the fact-checkers wake up. Today, there is no limit to how many pitchforks he can put into the hands of the virtual mob because social media allows it to swell to unlimited sizes, spreading his words far and wide, for free.

People around Trump are also blameworthy. Some among us have too readily accepted the president's offers to start Twitter wars to denigrate critics opposed to the administration's policies, while others actively seek him out and ask Trump to send raw voltage into the news feeds of his followers in order to light up a new cause. The president knows he can make people angry about anything. Everyone on his team has seen it happen, and people try to take advantage of it.

The real threat is when the madness bleeds over from the digital world into the real one, as it does at Trump events. You should see the West Wing before a rally. It's buzzing like a pre-game locker room. Trump doesn't travel to these arena-sized events to talk policy. He goes to rile up the crowd with pull-no-punches attacks on his enemies. With a Marine One helicopter waiting on the South Lawn, aides might be trying to tell him about a stock market development, but he's not hearing it. He's in the zone and thinking about bombastic things to say from the podium tonight. Trump might pause the meeting to road test an incendiary one-liner by calling a confidant to see if it really stings.

Watch any Trump rally. Whether through chants of "Lock her up!" or "Send her back!" our president arms audiences with weaponized language. At an event in Florida, Trump asked the crowd how to deal with illegal immigrants. "How do you stop these people?" he asked, his frustration visibly mounting while talking about the challenges at the border. "Shoot them!" one rally-goer cried. Rather than temper the suggestion, the president smiled and chuckled. "That's only in the Panhandle you can get away with that statement."

Defenders have scoffed at the idea that the president incites clannish hatred. At the aforementioned rally, they say, he prefaced his question by actually clarifying that the United States *couldn't* use weapons to fend off immigrant caravans. "We can't. I would never do that," Trump conceded, but those are the types of tongue-in-cheek statements he makes when he actually *does* want to do something.

In fact, it was Trump himself the previous year who suggested shooting immigrants found crossing the border. Yes, shooting them, real human beings, with bullets from guns held by members of our armed forces. "They are throwing rocks viciously and violently," he said, discussing an incoming caravan of people, most of whom were fleeing poverty. They'd been on the march for weeks and had gotten past Mexican authorities. "We are not going to put up with that. If they want to throw rocks at our military, our military fights back. I told them to consider it a rifle. When they throw rocks like they did at the Mexico military and police, I say consider it a rifle."

Some people listening thought this was just another Trump riff that carried him away for a moment, but it wasn't rhetoric. It wasn't facetious. He wanted it to happen. He'd deployed US troops to the border because he was trying to show a "tougher" response. Trump didn't want to murder innocent people, but he thought injuring a few immigrants would serve as a warning to others. "Why not?" he asked advisors. Defense Department officials, in full panic, picked up the phone to forcefully remind the White House about the actual rules of engagement for our troops, which did not include opening fire on unarmed civilians.

At a minimum, Trump's language is alienating in a way that feeds hateful groupthink. It's hard for my fellow Republicans to acknowledge this because the media is so sensationalistic. Television talking heads always assume the president's actions are bigoted, hyperventilating about everything he does. Trust me, I feel tempted to write them off, too, but there is no avoiding the fact that his words have a striking undertone of racial animus. Is this so hard to believe?

Fellow Republicans called candidate Trump a "race-baiting xenophobic bigot" in the presidential campaign. Do those now-silent Republicans believe the magic of the Oval Office has somehow transformed the man into a champion for racial tolerance? Nothing has changed. Whatever you think of Donald Trump, his views are alienating and deeply ingrained. When the president talks about people he wants to keep out of America, he tends to bring up Latin America, Africa, or Middle Eastern nations. When he tells the public about places he loves—countries whose citizens he would happily welcome in large numbers—he tends to talk about European nations, especially white, wealthy Nordic countries. I still don't think he's a hardline racist, but draw your own conclusions.

Extremists are hijacking the president's rhetoric to promote their movements. The killer responsible for the deadly mass shooting at an El Paso Walmart, for example, wrote that he was "defending my country from cultural and ethnic replacement brought on by an [Hispanic] invasion"—an "invasion" that Trump speaks about almost daily. Is the president culpable in such heinous acts? Absolutely not, but he *is* responsible for setting the tone on divisive issues, for failing to choose his words carefully, and for fostering a climate of intimidation that can cultivate violence.

Steady Staters were cognizant of this. Before a major speech or event, some would try to moderate the tone as best they could by editing the president's public remarks. The effect was limited by the reality that Trump constantly goes off script. Afterward advisors might suggest to the president that he steer clear of a phrase or idea that could be perceived as a dog whistle to hate groups, or that was particularly offensive to an ethnic or religious minority. That doesn't happen a whole lot anymore, and the fiery rhetoric is getting more atrocious.

Nearly three-quarters of Americans surveyed agreed that "elected officials should avoid using heated language because it could encourage violence." It can, it does, and it has. They should also consider whether it could result in what our Founders feared: democracy's foundations being ripped apart by mob rule.

Speaking to a group of Civil War veterans in 1875, Ulysses S. Grant speculated that if ever the nation were torn apart again, it would not be split North versus South along the infamous Mason-Dixon Line, the geographic boundary that separated free states and slave states. He surmised that in the future the dividing line would be reason itself, with intelligence on one side and ignorance on the other. Grant was a student of history. He knew that in societies where truth comes under attack, the fertile soil is tilled for violent conflict. Austrian philosopher Karl Popper took it a step further, writing, "The more we try to return to the heroic age of tribalism, the more surely do we arrive at the Inquisition, at the Secret Police, and at a romanticized gangsterism," a horrible degeneration that begins with the push of a domino—"the suppression of reason and truth."

It comes as a surprise to no one that political tribalism is surging in America. Our self-selected groups are becoming more partisan and less inclusive than ever before. Today we have a digital Mason-Dixon Line. It is splitting our country right down the middle, all the way to the household level. Donald Trump is not its sole cause. The line was drawn by the disruptive effects of technology and the fundamentals of human psychology, but the president's demagoguery has worsened the problem. His words are reshaping who we are.

An early colonist branded America a "shining city on a hill," an image that has defined our country for centuries since. In his farewell address, Ronald Reagan added more color to the analogy, saying the United States was "a tall, proud city built on rocks stronger than oceans, windswept, God-blessed, and teeming with people of all kinds living in harmony and peace…and if there had to be city walls, the walls had doors and the doors were open to anyone with the will and the heart to get here." Unfortunately, if we continue in our current direction, America will start to look more like the scene of "American carnage" the president said it was on his first day in office. He is debasing our national conversation to that level, and it's up to us whether it's acceptable.

If Trump's actions have turned the US government into one of his failed businesses, his rhetoric is turning our national stage into one of his reality television shows. It is no longer a preeminent forum for the debate of high-minded issues. The stage is fast becoming a drama-soaked series following the misadventures of a business tycoon navigating Washington in search of power and popularity, stirring up new controversies to capture the short attention span of a glass-eyed, zombie-like mob of spectators. They are desperate to be entertained, willing to be fooled, and easily provoked toward infighting by his unseemly antics. If you feel sick watching this production, imagine what it's like to be a part of the cast.

CHAPTER 7

Apologists

"The President hears a hundred voices telling him that he is the greatest man in the world. He must listen carefully indeed to hear the one voice that tells him he is not."

—*Harry Truman*

Donald Trump was the unwanted candidate. Ask any official serving in the Trump administration today if he or she supported the real-estate magnate when he threw his hat into the ring. In an unguarded moment, chances are they will tell you no. Many will admit that, in the field of seventeen Republican primary candidates in the 2016 race, Donald Trump was their seventeenth pick, dead last. His candidacy was a stunt.

When people don't have to take something seriously, they ridicule it. When they *do* have to take it seriously, they criticize it. As a candidate, Trump was ridiculed from the start. His comments were outlandish, so it was easy to joke about him. The mockery became feverish critique as soon as onlookers realized he might have a shot at the nomination. It was a clown car that became a slow-motion auto accident—funny at first, but soon horrific.

As we've discussed, conservative commentators tended to be candidate Trump's most formidable critics. They didn't believe he was one of their own. Elected officials in the Republican Party were even harsher.

New Jersey governor Chris Christie said the candidate lacked the credentials for the nation's highest office. "We do not need reality TV in the Oval Office right now," Christie lamented. "President of the United States is not a place for an entertainer."

Senator Ted Cruz lambasted him as a "narcissist" and "utterly amoral." Cruz argued that voters could not afford to elect someone so unfocused and social-media-obsessed. "I think in terms of a commander in chief, we ought to have someone who isn't springing out of bed to tweet in a frantic response to the latest polls."

Representative Jim Jordan, a leading conservative and one of the founders of the Freedom Caucus in the US House, wished Republicans in Congress had acted sooner to "avoid creating this environment" that allowed someone like candidate Trump to rise.

Texas governor Rick Perry labeled Trump "a cancer on conservatism" and a threat to the nation's future. "The White House has been occupied by giants," Rick noted. "But from time to time it is sought by the small-minded—divisive figures propelled by anger, and appealing to the worst instincts in the human condition." Perry said the businessman was peddling a "carnival act that can be best described as Trumpism: a toxic mix of demagoguery, mean-spiritedness, and nonsense" and that he was running on "division and resentment."

Senator Lindsey Graham told American voters: "This is not about who we nominate anymore as Republicans as much as it is who we are." He bemoaned that the party had not taken the long-shot candidate more seriously. "Any time you leave a bad idea or a dangerous idea alone, any time you ignore what could become an evil force, you wind up regretting it." The senator said he would not vote for the man, whom he called a "jackass" and a "kook." Those who know Lindsey understand that he wasn't using those words lightly. He meant them.

John Thune, one of the top-ranking Republicans in the Senate, expressed reservations throughout the race, but after the *Access Hollywood* scandal, he said the party no longer needed its candidate. "Donald Trump should withdraw and Mike Pence should be our nominee effective immediately," he tweeted in the wake of the scandal, with only weeks until the vote.

Many other elected conservatives chimed in throughout the campaign, calling the Republican nominee a "bigot," "misogynist," "liar," "unintelligent," "inarticulate," "dangerous," "fraud," "bully," and "unfit" for the presidency.

One Republican had especially blunt words as the clock ticked down to Election Day. He said he only supported Trump out of antipathy toward Hillary Clinton. "I'm doing so despite the fact that I think he's a terrible human being." Donald Trump is "absolutely *not*" a role model, the conservative leader declared. In fact, he is "[one] of the most flawed human beings ever to run for president in the history of the country."

The speaker was South Carolina congressman Mick Mulvaney. Roughly twenty-four months later, Mick would become Donald Trump's third chief of staff.

Apologists

Roman emperor Marcus Aurelius wrote what might be described as one of the earliest and most incisive "self-help" books of all time. Book Two of the tome opens with this advice:

> When you wake up in the morning, tell yourself: The people I deal with today will be meddling, ungrateful, arrogant, dishonest, jealous, and surly. They are like this because they can't tell good from evil. But I have seen the beauty of good, and the ugliness of evil, and have recognized that the wrongdoer has a nature related to my own...and so none of them can hurt me. No one can implicate me in ugliness.

Trump appointees would be wise to tape the emperor's words at their bedsides, for life has gotten uglier inside the administration. Looking right and left, we can see the Steady Staters are mostly gone. What remains are more defenders than do-gooders in the political ranks; obsequious pleasers outnumber thoughtful public servants. One of the most visible signs of the devolution is the unwillingness of people around the president to stand up to him.

It's important that advisors speak truth to

power. Presidents have enough flatterers in their midst. What they need more than anything are people willing to present unvarnished facts and to challenge bad decisions. This is essentially what the Steady State tried to do. If advisors feed "spin" to the president instead, it's a triple loss. The aide fails in his or her duty, the commander in chief is poorly served, and the country is worse off for it. Further still, making decisions based on *fiction* and not *fact* can create new problems for a president to solve, becoming a vicious cycle of misinformation-turned-mistake.

The Trump story is briskly moving into a fictional universe. Sometimes aides are afraid to tell President Trump what is really happening, or they buoy his belief that he can take actions that, in reality, he cannot. The result is that President Trump makes more untrue statements than he would otherwise and takes ill-advised courses of action detrimental to the nation. Staff don't want to deliberately mislead him. More often than not, they make these mistakes because they want to seem supportive of Trump's agenda, even when it doesn't comport with reality. I can't overstate how precarious it is for a president's advisors to become an assemblage of servants.

Consider President Trump's response to Hurricane Dorian, when he incorrectly stated that Alabama was in the storm's path at a time when it wasn't. The president refused to admit he was wrong and his information was outdated. He spent days unloading at the White House to anyone in earshot, insisting he was right about where it *could* have gone and whom it *could* have hit. The fury didn't take long to spill into public view. Trump whipped out an old poster board of the storm track in the Oval Office, which had been marked up with a Sharpie to make it look like the storm was still projected to hit Alabama. Trump was mocked further, which infuriated him more. All the while Americans in the storm's path wondered what the hell their president was doing. I could only shake my head.

Rather than urge him to issue a short correction, too many aides in the West Wing were eager to help him perpetuate the lie. Trump made phone calls to get the answers he wanted. They heeded the call. He told them to issue statements disputing reality. They did. He asked for data points to make it seem like he'd been right. They complied. By the end, it was like a game of Twister gone wrong; the truth was so tied up in knots, no one knew what the hell we were talking about anymore. The poor folks at the weather agencies were badly demoralized by their first exposure to the common-yet-frightening White House spin cycle.

A conservative time traveler from 2016 would find the whole charade amusing, if it weren't so serious. "Didn't you fools hear the warnings?" he or she might say. "Republicans anticipated this. We predicted this is precisely what a Trump adminis-tration would look like!" They would be correct, of course. GOP leaders were accurate in describing the man and prophetic in forecasting the outcome of this presidency. The validity of their words hasn't changed. What changed is their minds.

Gun Fight

Donald Trump brought an assortment of hangers-on into the White House. He collected assistants throughout the years, building an island of misfit apprentices. During the campaign, he gathered more. His operation was a magnet for third-rate talent, attracting the political equivalent of ama-teur day traders, the kind who liked to walk the line between risk-taking and indictments. They all tried to come into the White House with Presi-dent Trump, but luckily, mature voices stepped in to push many of the lackeys aside. For a time it worked. But in Trump's world, the descent of good people is as absolute as the law of gravity. The rise of the Steady State was followed by its inevitable fall.

Today a third category of advisors is ascendant: the Apologists.

The shift occurred at the end of year two. As the Steady State crumbled, White House budget director Mick Mulvaney was tapped as acting chief of staff, coming a long way from vehement Trump critic to close presidential aide. Despite telling colleagues he was not interested in the job, he angled for months to get it. Mulvaney is a survivor. He saw opportunity as John Kelly's star dimmed. The acting chief confided in friends not long after taking the position that he didn't understand why Kelly loathed it so much. The perks were great (he became especially fond of visiting Camp David), and he got to be in the thick of it whenever he wanted, while stepping back when he didn't.

Mulvaney brought a new approach to managing the West Wing. He didn't manage it. His guiding maxim was: *Let Trump be Trump.* Mick's outlook—don't challenge the president's impulses, just make them work—represented a sharp departure from his predecessor. No longer would officials play back-in-the-box with the president's awful ideas. Instead, we were urged to focus on making bad ideas more palatable, to soften their rough edges. This kept the president happy and his acting chief of staff out of Trump's line of fire. The only problem with the approach is that Trump has not changed since the time Mulvaney blasted him as a "terrible human being." So, in effect, Mulvaney's *raison d'être* is to help a "terrible human being" be maybe a little less terrible, if he can swing it. If not, well, that's okay, too.

With the guardrails gone, "year three" of the Trump administration might as well have been announced as "season three." Old controversies previously averted struck back with a vengeance, and the cast of characters grew seedier. Aside from the Syria withdrawal, the president resumed his "shutdown" mantra. With fewer and fewer aides to persuade him otherwise—and a chief of staff eager to accommodate—Trump decided to close the government and demand more money for his border wall. Few in the administration or in Congress supported the plan. It was senseless for a variety of reasons, namely that it didn't appear the president had the leverage he thought he did.

The result was a foreseeable disaster. Nobody in the White House had a plan for ending the impasse, and nobody wanted to be responsible for finding one. "This place is so fucked up," an official on the ad hoc shut-down team complained weeks into the government closure, as everyone else watched helplessly. "There is literally no one in charge here." As evidence of the bedlam, Vice President Pence was scheduled to lead White House negotiations to cut a deal. Rather than sit down with members of Congress who could broker a path forward, a meeting was arranged between Pence and their staff members. The legislators were out of town on recess. It was an embarrassing display that Pence had to endure with a smile. He was, unfortunately, used to that.

Pressure mounted on the president to give up. Government employees were missing paychecks, and even junior aides around the White House fretted about making ends meet. Many of us thought the whole ordeal was a waste of time and worried about the compounding effects across government. Information was shared with the president about the growing consequences of a prolonged government closure. Then the media reported that US airports would soon take a hit, snarling travel across the country. That did it. Shortly after, the president caved and reopened the government with little to show for the debacle. Trump didn't secure the "billions" of dollars he demanded for his wall and wound up with a political black eye to kick off the new Congress—a very bad and very avoidable start to the year.

We've continued down this dirt road, with one unforced error after another. Decisions that had previously been teed up carefully for the president, such as the future of the US presence in Afghanistan, are now being shanked into the rough. Donald Trump is so anxious to withdraw from the country that he nearly brought Taliban leaders to Camp David for a summit to agree to a deal on the eve of the September 11 anniversary, infuriating Trump appointees who weren't informed. Remember, we're talking about the same people who harbored the terrorist group that murdered nearly three thousand Americans and who are responsible for killing or injuring hundreds of US soldiers. They don't deserve to step on US soil, let alone be welcomed by the president of the United States at a retreat used to huddle with American allies. Yet there are fewer people left to reject the folly of these ideas, and those that do are written off by the president as disloyal.

The demise of the Steady State also means the culture of the executive branch has returned to a darker place. Infighting, which surged in the early months of the administration but eventually leveled out, has returned with a literal vengeance. You may think you have an ally, only to find the same person talked to the president about your potential firing. Ambitious staffers are jockeying for position as more people are either purged or flee the building. Vacancies mean potential promotions, creating an incentive for overzealous climbers to undercut their colleagues in order to advance. Staffers threw sharp elbows to make their way into Mulvaney's office, and in places such as the Pentagon, mid-level political appointees fought for jobs to get in close proximity to General Mattis's replacement, acting secretary Pat Shanahan, and then later to his replacement's replacement, Mark Esper, who took the job when Shanahan was unceremoniously kicked out by Trump.

First-time hires are naive about the level of drama until they encounter it. I remember a new Trump appointee attempting to assert independence from a questionable White House policy by leaking internal deliberations to the press to distance himself. The problem was that he threw a more veteran and ruthless political staffer under the bus. "That was a bad move. He brought a knife to a gun fight," a communications aide said after reading the news article. "That fucker will be dead by morning." If the Trump administration is good at anything, it knows how to eat its own.

The cannibalistic culture is deterring good people from coming on board. Mick has struggled to source qualified, outside candidates for essential positions that would have been sought by big-name politicians across the country only a few years ago. Making matters worse, Trump prefers to go with his gut on new appointees. He is too impatient to vet candidates to determine whether they are the right fit for the job.

The result is that the president's tweet-picked nominees shrink in the spotlight and appear unqualified—because they often are. Consider the time the president announced Texas congressman John Ratcliffe would be his nominee as director of National Intelligence. The congressman had no real intelligence background. His only qualification was that he was a staunch defender of the president on television. Ratcliffe withdrew himself when it became apparent that the Republican-led Senate didn't share Trump's enthusiasm.

With the president's four-year term hitting the homestretch, gun fights and rivalries are thinning the herd. As a result, the administration has lost its real leaders, and unsavory figures are racing to the forefront. The public doesn't recognize many of their names yet, but they will eventually. You will see them get subpoenaed and watch them testify. History will record the rise of the Apologists, and, one day, perhaps one day soon, chronicle their fall.

Why the Worst Get on Top

In the midst of the Second World War, Austrian intellectual Friedrich Hayek published *The Road to Serfdom*, describing how free societies descend into totalitarianism. Hayek's tenth chapter, "Why the Worst Get on Top," offered a description for how "the unscrupulous are likely to be more successful in a society tending toward totalitarianism."

It's not accurate to say Donald Trump is a dictator. Commentators who make such claims shouldn't be taken seriously. However, it's fair to say the president possesses clear authoritarian tendencies like very few presidents before him. Trump's attempt to mimic the strongmen he admires has certainly led us to take steps down the road Hayek mentions.

The Austrian thinker listed three main reasons why, over time, an authoritarian personality is likely to be surrounded not by the best "but rather by the worst elements of any society." President

Trump's inner circle has increasingly checked each of those boxes.

First, Hayek explained, an autocrat needs a group with questionable morals. The cohort will also tend to be undereducated. "If we wish to find a high degree of uniformity in outlook, we have to descend to the regions of lower moral and intellectual standards where the more primitive instincts prevail." Check.

Second, the autocrat must expand the size of the subservient group. He "must gain the support of the docile and gullible, who have no strong convictions of their own but are ready to accept a ready-made system of values if it is only drummed into their ears sufficiently loudly and frequently." Check.

Finally, Hayek said, authoritarian types need to weld the group together by appealing to their basic human weaknesses. "It seems to be easier for people to agree on a negative program—on the hatred of an enemy, on the envy of the better off—than on any positive task. The contrast between the 'we' and the 'they' is consequently always employed by those who seek the allegiance of huge masses." Check.

The end result is the core team will be faithful in implementing the leader's policies. "To be a useful assistant in the running of a totalitarian state," Hayek wrote, "it is not enough that a man should be prepared to accept specious justification of vile deeds." He must be prepared to carry them out. "Since it is the supreme leader who alone determines the ends, his instruments must have no moral convictions of their own. They must, above all, be unreservedly committed to the person of the leader." Ultimately, their willingness to act in ways they know are wrong becomes their route to a promotion.

Hayek's characterization doesn't apply to everyone who serves in the Trump administration, yet there are echoes in his words of what has happened to our team. Unquestioning followers have floated to the top, stitched together by the president's enmity toward "others"—criminals, immigrants, enemies in the media, job-stealers. His internal coalition stays united because of what they stand against, not for. They clap politely when he talks about something like supporting America's veterans with better care, but they roar with laughter and approval when he blasts a left-wing first-term congresswoman from New York City, an evil liberal trying to revive socialism in America.

The real question is, what motivates Trump's Apologists to support him even when his behavior is wrong? Why do his boosters take to the airwaves, performing verbal gymnastics to defend immoral statements or conduct? Some of them are the same people who stood on the train tracks with their hands in the air trying to stop Trump from becoming president. *So what turned them into Trump's human shields?* Hayek's words above offer a partial explanation, but I want to flesh them out further. During my time in the Trump administration, I have witnessed three primary motivations for what a passerby would call brainwashing. Power, tribal allegiance, and fear.

Trump Apologists see him as a means to personal influence and advancement. They want to be close to power. They are eager for stature they wouldn't gain otherwise and are willing to excuse Trump's actions to get it. Even then-candidate Trump's most pointed critics, such as Texas governor Rick Perry, were willing to cast aside their existential warnings about the future of the country in order to snag comfortable positions in his cabinet. Perry is an actual conservative who was the longest-serving governor in his state's history. Now he doesn't spend too much time extolling conservative values and largely tries to avoid the president's attention or ire inside the administration. Others pretend they weren't interested in joining but secretly wish they'd been picked for similar positions.

Apologists

For some appointees, the "power" they want is financial. Aides openly discuss how one political position or another will translate into post-government dollars. Some believe an ongoing connection to Trump World offers opportunities for a small windfall in the political afterlife. Perhaps they can go work for his company, or maybe Jared and Ivanka will take aides with them into the private sector and build something with their star power. These are hardly the motives the American people expect to animate their public servants. Others who do leave the administration are often bought off with a high salary at the Trump campaign or at a super PAC to pacify them. So far, that's worked pretty well, becoming standard practice for President Trump, who dangles future offers for disaffected lieutenants to keep them quiet. Omarosa Manigault, who claimed she was offered a six-figure salary to stay on the team, was a vocal exception.

For many elected Republicans, abandoning their concerns and supporting the president has brought them the power of influence. They can ring up Trump when they need a few minutes on the phone to talk about their pet project, fly with him on Air Force One to be photographed at a major event, or get name-checked in an approving Trump tweet with a hundred thousand "likes." It

317

will help them shore up their base and avoid primary challengers. Because it's easier to win with the bully on your side.

Blind devotion is another factor. The president demands unyielding loyalty from his subordinates, even if that runs afoul of their job descriptions. "I need loyalty. I expect loyalty," he told Jim Comey. He has the same expectation for many other positions that are supposed to be semi-independent from the political sway of the White House, whether it's a spy agency head or the Fed chair. These roles have autonomy for good reason. Not in Donald Trump's mind. He wants to see signs of personal submission, and he gets it, or the other person is in the firing line.

We were all unnerved by an early cabinet meeting, when one by one members of the administration took turns offering extravagant praise of the commander in chief on national television. A more secure person would have called a halt to the cheesy compliments—"We thank you for the opportunity and the blessing you've given us," then chief of staff Reince Priebus gushed. Donald Trump basked in it, like a potentate accepting offerings from grateful peasants. If you go back and watch the video, you'll notice a few cabinet members declined to offer personal tribute, instead praising their workforces. They withheld the Trump flattery, and now they are gone.

One superb political study out of Brigham Young University found that "group loyalty is the stronger motivator of opinion than are any ideological principles." Many people around the president and in the GOP support him *because* he is at the helm, not because of what he believes. In fact, they support him *regardless* of what he believes. He has created a true cult of personality. Whether he is right or wrong, the tribe must protect him, even if that means forsaking their principles.

Finally, some are motivated by fear—of criticism, of reprisals, and of job loss. A culture of fear is what we would expect from a leader with authoritarian tendencies. In his own words, Trump embraces fear as a management tool. He enjoys keeping aides on their toes with *Game of Thrones* intrigue about possible terminations, or by threatening allies with severe repercussions if they break with him. Republicans have seen the consequences when someone takes on the party's Goliath. He takes no prisoners.

Potential defectors saw what happened when Trump set out to ruin his former senior aide Steve Bannon after Bannon spilled unflattering details in a book about the president. Aides were banned from speaking to him and ordered to go on television to denounce him. Trump sought to destroy his role at Breitbart News, his support from Republican donors, and his friendships with anyone seeking to do business with the administration. Trump will go after family members of turncoats, too, as he did with relatives of Michael Cohen and Anthony Scaramucci.

Thus, the weak-natured in the administration and the GOP have become more compliant.

Smiling and Nodding

How do you identify a Trump Apologist? They often display a telltale trait: smiling and nodding at the wrong time.

Put them in a room with the president and watch as he strings together unrelated sentences, as his tone changes, as his face contorts, and as he declares he is going to do something very, very good (but that reasonable people know is *not* good at all, and perhaps very bad). Watch as he gestures his hands to those around the room, enlisting them by extension in his declaration, whether they willingly endorse it or not. Then scan the room. The bobbing heads and forced grins are Apologists. You can see for yourself on television because the president invites the press to cover these conversations, as a means to display his total dominance of those around him.

There are two separate types of unsavory Trump appointee. Both belong to the same *genus*, the Apologist, defined by their shared willingness to excuse the inexcusable. But each is its own *species* with distinctive characteristics. The first species is the Sycophant. The second is the Silent Abettor. The intermingling motives—power, tribalism, and fear—are what keep both species nodding in agreement.

The Sycophant is a true believer. He or she fell for the president's message right away and admires Trump to the point of literal brand loyalty. They would purchase Trump Steaks or Trump Vodka if they could (no longer on sale). If he produces it, the Sycophants will buy it. Today, they patronize the Trump International Hotel down the street from the White House, where they lap up drinks as thirstily as they do the president's talking points. When he mocks people less powerful, they laugh; when he comes up with a derogatory slur for an opponent, they call him "brilliant" for appealing to the masses in a way no one else can. The Sycophant's motives are a combination of "power" and "tribalism," which is why, when the president asks them to do something wrong-headed, they won't flinch. His ethics are their ethics.

You often see these folks on television. Almost everyone gets asked to do media on behalf of the president at some point. Most of those who agree to do so, though not all of them, are the Sycophants. They will happily carry Trump's toxic water for him, indifferent to the beating taken by their reputations for defending untruths and inventing new ones. To some of the best of them, it might start as a genuine desire to push back against unfair reporting and to promote the president's better policies. Before long it becomes a way of life. You cross a moral and logical Rubicon to serve Trump's media cravings. I haven't seen anyone who has made this journey ever come back.

The Silent Abettor is a lousier form of Apologist than the cheerleading Sycophant. At least the Sycophant, however delusional, *believes* he or she is acting virtuously, living up to values of Trumpism. The Silent Abettors know what's happening is wrong. They are aware an impetuous man is presiding over the executive branch. They watch him flip-flop with the change of a channel, or unveil shoddy decisions instantaneously with a few keystrokes, CAPS LOCK on, extra exclamation points for emphasis. And they say nothing. Their motivations are a combination of "power" and "fear," and they will do what President Trump wants because they have subordinated their beliefs to a short-term, naked self-interest. The Silent Abettor is a species that is all too abundant in the Trump administration.

While it is indeed disturbing that we've elevated someone so ill-informed as Trump to the nation's highest office, what's depressing is how many people around him and in the Republican Party are remaining quiet when their voices are needed to make the difference between poor policy and good government. They don't necessarily need to speak out publicly against the president to have an impact. They just need to speak up in his presence, in the meetings that count, or among fellow administration officials. Silent Abettors should realize saying something *is* in their self-interest because, if they don't, they'll be the next ones at a microphone defending an unconscionable decision.

Trump Apologists will be the first sent out to denounce this book. The president will direct them to deny any of the characterizations or episodes contained herein. They are used to it, as they have been denying stories they know are true for years. I wonder, though, would those same people stick by their denials about the reckless and politically charged official actions the president has taken if they were put under oath? I suppose that's another question for Congress to consider.

Members of the informal Steady State are not guilt-free in this. We all wish we did more to confront wrong-headed decisions early on. There were times we could have acted and didn't. Still, many members of this cohort have found ways to push back against what's inexcusable. That might mean sucking it up and getting into an argument with Trump or one of his close allies. It might mean alerting others about what was coming down the line, or it might mean publicly breaking with the president on an issue.

Those who keep their heads down will live to regret it. Cautionary tales are plentiful. Go no further than the president's homeland security leaders, who, in a sickening display of bad judgment, conceded to a policy that increased the number of children ripped from the arms of their parents at the US-Mexico border. It left a stain on their reputations, their department, and the country. It was a seminal moment of Trumpism gone too far and a lesson for others. Trump's character rubs off on people who came into government to do what is right. Before long, they find themselves supporting and defending policies they never imagined they would.

I know more than a handful of people who set "redlines" for their time in the Trump administration, boundaries they would refuse to cross or behavior they wouldn't tolerate from the commander in chief. They would quit, they told friends, if those conditions were triggered. Then I've watched the same people breeze right over those redlines, shamefully rationalizing and justifying themselves along the way.

The rise of Apologists inside the Trump administration should matter to voters. These people are his clones, displaying many of the traits we've come to detest in Trump and carrying his marching order into all areas of government. They validate him when they should be challenging him to think critically. Voters should take into account the major policy decisions the Apologists will help the president make if he's reelected, as well as the caustic behaviors and prejudices these aides will be reinforcing in Trump's ethos. Those who ignore it are effectively joining the death march of thoughtless followers, smiling and nodding along the way.

The Crickets of Capitol Hill

If you've walked around the US Capitol Building on a summer night, you know it's one of the most beautiful sights in America. The grounds are lined with greenery and dotted with hundreds of trees from across the United States. According to the architect of the Capitol, the landscaping is deliberately designed to "hide views of the Capitol except from specific angles to show off the building's architecture at its most majestic and inspiring vantage points." It does that and more. During the day this place is frenetic, enveloped by the sounds of our national discussion, but at night, it is quiet. You can hear little more than the crickets as you admire the brightly lit white dome, a citadel rising above the forest around it.

Congress is where the presidency is fiercely examined and ardently debated. Legislators, regardless of party, have an obligation to monitor the executive branch. They should do so fairly and respectfully, but above all they should do so. Unfortunately, on one side of the aisle, it sounds like nighttime on Capitol Hill. All you hear is the crickets. Republicans are hesitant to criticize the president when he deserves it, and if they can't applaud him, they just go quiet.

More so than Trump's current and former aides, it is important for voices on Capitol Hill and in the Republican Party to speak up about the president's conduct. These people will continue to lead the country long after Trump is gone. They should be the umpires of the executive branch, calling the balls and strikes as they see them. Yet Congress has been overtaken by the invasive species, too, the Sycophants and the Silent Abettors.

All of the GOP officials I quoted at the outset of this chapter have since evolved from critics to Apologists.

For instance, Senator Ted Cruz, who once labeled Trump immoral and ill-suited for the presidency, now tells rally-goers that the president's decisions are "bold" and "courageous"—that he's proud "to have worked hand in hand with President Trump." Representative Jim Jordan, who lamented the environment that allowed Donald Trump to rise within the party in the first place, is one of his Capitol Hill attack dogs, taking to cable news to champion the president's record. Trump returns the praise. "What a great defender he has been," he said of Jordan, calling the congressman "a brave, tough cookie."

Senator Lindsey Graham, who said he'd never vote Trump, equating his candidacy with a "dangerous idea" that morphed into an "evil force," told interviewers a few months after the inauguration: "I am like the happiest dude in America right now." He said the president and his team are what he'd "been dreaming of for eight years." The senator was positively giddy about Trump's foreign policy. "I am all in. Keep it up, Donald. I'm sure you're watching."

The same transformation has happened to more public servants than I can count. They've forgotten their oath is to the US Constitution, not to a man nor to a political base. Consequently, the Oval Office has become a welcome sanctuary to members of Congress who say the magic words: "Yes, Mr. President." Those who stand up to him, a small number, to be sure, aren't welcomed back. The servile attitudes are a danger to the presidency, to the Congress as an independent branch, and to our democracy.

Think about the time the president dismissed a string of poor countries as "shitholes" in a private meeting with Cabinet officials, aides, and members of Congress. The public outcry over Trump's remarks—he was quoted as saying, "Why do we need more Haitians, take them out," and that we needed less immigrants from "all these shithole countries" in places like Africa in favor of places like Norway—led to a prompt denial from Trump himself. "That was not the language used," he tweeted. Trump demanded aides and allies to support him on this, which they did. Former homeland security chief Kirstjen Nielsen told the press she did not "hear" him use those words, and Senators Tom Cotton and David Perdue went on television to flatly deny that he said "shithole" when referring to the mostly black nations. First they attacked Democrats for misrepresenting the meeting, and then it was reported that they believed Trump said "shit *house*" rather than "shit *hole,*" which allowed them to deny it on a technicality.

Of course, everyone in the room knew that Trump had used crude words to describe those foreign countries. We've heard him make comments like that all the time, and he's actually harkened back to the term "shithole" in private since. So why did people go out and pretend otherwise? To please their patron. Ironically, after forcing people to stand behind Trump's denial, the White House basically conceded that Trump used vulgar language about the poor non-white countries, with Sarah Sanders telling reporters, "No one here is going to pretend like the president is always politically correct."

History has shown the consequences of a climate where officials focus more on attending to "the principal" than heeding their own first principles. Studying in London in the mid-1700s, one of America's soon-to-be Founding Fathers, John Dickinson, was struck by how a follower mentality had infected Great Britain's once-revered political capital. "Such is the complacency these great men have for the smiles of their prince," he wrote of English public servants, "that they will gratify every desire of ambition and power at the expense of truth, reason, and their country." The environment led to widespread corruption, disputed elections, and a nation that ultimately went to war with itself. Donald Trump is America's smiling prince.

Republican detractors today are a dwindling band. Those who stick their necks out deserve credit, though they've rarely gotten it from Trump voters. On the Senate side, Mitt Romney issued a *Washington Post* op-ed critical of the president and vowed to maintain an ongoing appraisal of Trump's conduct, writing, "A president should demonstrate the essential qualities of honesty and integrity, and elevate the national discourse with

comity and mutual respect…And it is in this prov-
ince where the incumbent's shortfall has been most
glaring." On the House side, Representative Justin Amash has been a staunch critic of the president and called on Americans to join in "rejecting
the partisan loyalties and rhetoric that divide and
dehumanize us." His attacks have isolated him
from the Republican Party, which he ultimately
announced he was leaving.

Some leading Republicans have sought to atone
for their past public support of Trump. Former
House Speaker Paul Ryan once said he would
never defend Trump, but he wound up having to
do so weekly as the top Republican in Congress.
Now out of office, he described his attitude toward
the president much more candidly with journalist
Tim Alberta:

> I told myself I gotta have a relationship
> with this guy to help him get his mind right.
> Because, I'm telling you, he didn't know *any-
> thing* about government…I wanted to scold
> him all the time. Those of us around him
> really helped to stop him from making bad
> decisions. All the time. We helped him make
> much better decisions, which were contrary
> to kind of what his knee-jerk reaction was.

A Warning

Ryan is the rare former official willing to speak up. Many have remained quiet outside of government, although their experiences align closely with those of the former Speaker. They share the concerns outlined in this book. They have more to add, if they'll find the courage. But even those who've dared to say something still feel deep down that it's not enough. Because it's not. No one is immune. Anyone aiding the Trump administration is, or was, one of his Apologists. They've all waited too long to speak out and haven't spoken forcefully enough. Myself included.

CHAPTER 8

We the Electorate

"Who will govern the governors? There is only one force in the nation that can be depended upon to keep the government pure and the governors honest, and that is the people themselves."

—*Thomas Jefferson*

The verdict is in. Despite some accomplishments, it's evident Donald Trump is behaving immorally, weakening the party he professes to lead, undermining democratic institutions, abandoning crucial US alliances, emboldening our adversaries, dividing Americans with hateful rhetoric and chronic dishonesty, and surrounding himself with people who will only reinforce his defects. It was easy to dismiss a pile of insider accounts about the severity of the situation. However, the pile is now a mountain, and the stories paint the portrait of a leader who handles the nation's affairs with persistent negligence. Donald Trump deserves to be fired.

Yes, top officials have frequently hit the brakes to forestall disastrous presidential decisions, but as I noted in the beginning of this book, my original thesis in the *New York Times* was dead wrong. Americans should not expect that his advisors can fix the situation. We cannot. The question is what to do next. There are good and bad approaches for handling the historic leadership failures emanating from the Executive Office of the President. We must address the second category first.

Firing a President

A psychological phenomenon is affecting a large portion of the country. Some call it "Trump Derangement Syndrome" (TDS). If this were a clinical diagnosis, it would best be characterized as the disturbance in normal cognitive function resulting in irrational animus toward the president of the United States. Said differently: people who hate Trump so much that they can't think straight. There is no doubt President Donald Trump is living rent-free in all of our heads. He occupies more daily mindshare, argument, and concern for the average American than any prior chief executive, but fever-ish consternation about a president shouldn't lead us to automatically pursue drastic measures.

Those who suffer from TDS have had dark fantasies for years about how Trump's tenure can be cut short. They've imagined he will be forced to resign for doing something so terrible that it shocks the conscience of the nation. They've prayed his cabinet will evict him by invoking emergency Constitutional provisions. They've yearned for him to be impeached and removed by the US Congress, or they've had other disgraceful thoughts that don't merit discussion whatsoever but which perhaps deserve a visit from the US Secret Service.

On this score, I want to speak to Trump's politi-cal opponents and his harshest critics, the ones who want him thrown out of office at any cost. I under-stand your frustration. I, too, have developed strong opinions about the president's performance and whether he deserves to continue leading our great nation. But when we engage in careless speculation about the president's ouster, we are promoting a level of anti-democratic behavior on par with the con-duct for which we are criticizing Trump. It's time to restate the obvious. Although Donald Trump is undoubtedly prone to contemptible behavior, we should not wish upon our nation the crisis of premature presidential expulsion. It might be how the story ends, but we must be reluctant to fire a president in non-electoral ways and should only consider doing so as an absolute last resort.

First, let's start with terrible misdeeds. Some people hope the president will do something so awful that he must resign immediately in the face of widespread popular discontent. A few senior members of Trump's team privately imagined the possibility. As one said, the president's inclinations are so bad that perhaps we should "give him enough rope" to entangle his own presidency. This wouldn't be hard. He is a factory that produces a steady stream of presidency-wrecking ideas. In that case, the advisor suggested letting him fire the special counsel and Justice Department leadership. He seemed eager enough to do it. If aides helped him follow his instincts, they speculated, it would lead to his downfall.

I find the proposition disturbing on its face. While the president has unquestionably engaged in conduct that is detrimental to our country, we should never encourage bad behavior only so we can punish it. For that reason, no one to my knowledge considered instigating such an outcome beyond making thoughtless comments. Steady Staters, or what's left of the group, feel obligated to keep the presidency on the rails and to dissuade Trump from taking self-destructive actions. The country deserves nothing less. To permit a wrong—or to encourage one—is to be culpable in it. For the health of our republic, we should never long for our president to act egregiously enough to inspire bipartisan masses to demand resignation.

Second: the Twenty-fifth Amendment. Although this is a dreadful idea, the concept was informally broached in conversations in Washington's halls of power. Trump's behavior became so erratic in the weeks following Jim Comey's firing and the appointment of the special counsel that a number of senior administration officials worried about his mental state. Deputy Attorney General Rod Rosenstein reportedly considered wearing a wire to his West Wing meetings to document the madness in the president's White House. Within days of Trump's "fire Mueller" demands, others in the administration were having the same quiet conversations. They asked themselves, "Is the president still fit for office?"

The Twenty-fifth Amendment is a Constitutional provision that deals with presidential succession in cases of resignation, removal, incapacitation,

or death. Specifically, Trump administration officials honed in on section 4:

> Whenever the Vice President and a
> majority of either the principal officers of
> the executive departments or of such other
> body as Congress may by law provide, trans-
> mit to the President pro tempore of the
> Senate and the Speaker of the House of Rep-
> resentatives their written declaration that
> the President is unable to discharge the
> powers and duties of his office, the Vice Pres-
> ident shall immediately assume the powers
> and duties of the office as Acting President.

In short, if Vice President Pence and a majority of the cabinet felt that Trump could no longer
discharge his duties, they could remove him from
office.

To be clear, this was *not* an action the president's cabinet was preparing (or prepared) to take.
However, the disarray was so severe—and concern
about Trump's temperament so pervasive—that
his lieutenants talked about what would happen if
the situation got worse. This included comparing
notes on a breaking point. What level of instability
warranted presidential removal? Was it debilitat-

ing cognitive impairment? Was it a reckless order that put the American people in danger? There's no handbook for these situations.

A back-of-the-envelope "whip count" was conducted of officials who were most concerned about the deteriorating situation. Names of cabinet-level officials were placed on a mental list. These were folks who, in the worst-case scenario, would be amenable to huddling discreetly in order to assess how bad the situation was getting. Any discussion of the Twenty-fifth Amendment was hushed and fleeting, because almost everyone concluded it was irresponsible to speculate about it at all.

I froze when I first heard someone suggest that we might be getting into "Twenty-fifth territory." That's pretty scary talk, I thought. At home that night, I imagined how the hypothetical scenario would play out. The majority of the cabinet would probably meet somewhere in secret, away from the White House. They would draft a letter to the leaders of Congress certifying the president was "unable to discharge the powers and duties of his office." Those gathered around the table would take a deep breath and pass the pen in silence, each signing a document they knew would become one of the most consequential in US history.

Once the majority of the cabinet signed, someone would pass a message to the vice president. He would be waiting elsewhere until he was certain there was sufficient support. Then he would make his choice. Mike Pence holds his cards close when it comes to his opinions about Trump, but if a majority of the cabinet was prepared to remove the president and elevate Pence—if the emergency was that serious—there is no doubt what he'd do. He would affix his name to the paper. Everyone would feel the gravity of the moment in their gut. Armored vehicles would race across town to the US Capitol Building, and a protected courier would walk the document into the hands of congressional leaders.

As I contemplated this scenario, that unwelcome visitor in the Trump administration—reason—took over.

I thought…And then what? President Trump would stroll out of the White House, take a bow, and get on a helicopter to head home? Doubtful. If the story didn't already sound like a B-movie, this is where it would become a horror film. Removal of the president by his own cabinet would be perceived as a coup. The end result would be unrest in the United States the likes of which we haven't seen since maybe the Civil War. Millions would not accept the outcome, perhaps including the president himself, and many would take to the streets on both sides. Violence would be almost inevitable. The ensuing strife would break us for years to come. Among other good reasons, that is why the option was not seriously contemplated. The whispered conversations about "the Twenty-fifth" ceased, though concerns about the president's temperament have remained.

Trump's critics would be smart to drop the idea, too. They should keep such fantasies to themselves, lest they further poison our already toxic discourse. In a democracy we don't overthrow our leaders when they're underperforming. That's for third-rate banana republics and police states. The Twenty-fifth Amendment should be reserved for scenarios when the commander in chief is truly unable to discharge his duties, not when we are dissatisfied with his performance.

Third: impeachment. As of this writing, we are living through the prospect. We should not relish it. Impeachment inquiries are painful for the country and our political system, as history has shown. We must refrain from politicizing the impeachment process by letting frustration with Trump cloud our judgment about the facts. Much of the evidence of wrongdoing is disturbing, from the president urging Ukraine to investigate one of his political rivals to examples of Trump's efforts to improperly influence the Russia investigation. It is the job of Congress to consider whether these actions rise to the level of "high crimes and misdemeanors" and whether they justify Trump's removal from office.

It's un-American to *hope* our president is guilty of "high crimes." Wishing the president to be branded a criminal and booted prematurely from office means wishing ever-greater division upon the United States. We can scarcely afford further disunion. That's why we must put aside our passions and allow the exercise to run its course. We should demand that our representatives approach the deliberations soberly, without political malice. An impeachment motivated by public anger above truth would set a precedent far worse than whatever poor conduct it sought to remedy. Democrats in Congress should not rush to judgment, and they are obligated to run a fair process in the House. Similarly, if the evidence points to criminality, Republicans must not resist justice because it is politically inconvenient. They must follow the facts where they lead.

While I cannot discuss the specifics surrounding the present allegations against the president involving Ukraine beyond what is in the public record, as a general proposition it should not surprise anyone that Donald Trump would act in a manner that is unbecoming of his office and possibly disqualifying. He has always acted impulsively to serve his interests over those of the United States. As I've noted, he has repeatedly concocted ways to break the law if it gets him what he wants. More stories remain to be told and will come out in the months and years ahead. His ideas are often resisted, but they prove that Trump is indifferent to the reasons why presidents shouldn't abuse their power for personal gain. When he is warned about the propriety or legality of his proposals, he is agitated—to the point that he has pushed out many of the senior people who've tried to protect him. He has few guardrails left. More worrisome, reelection will convince him he is freer than ever to put his self-interest above the national interest.

Donald Trump's record is troubling. At some point, aspects of it might be found to have violated his oath of office. Unless and until that happens, though, all of the above courses of action are undesirable ways to fire a president. One option—and one option only—stands above the rest as the ultimate way to hold Trump accountable.

The People Themselves

In an anonymous essay designed to whip up support for the draft of the US Constitution, Alexander Hamilton wrote, "...the Executive should be independent for his continuance in office on all but the people themselves." No other political force should decide whether he stays or goes, save for exceptional circumstances. There is a single right way, prescribed by the architects of this country, for holding our leaders to account. It is as elegant as it is blunt. It is the transmission line for all power in our political system, determining who gains, retains, and loses authority. It is the election.

The people are the best and most legitimate recourse for our present political dilemma. The democratic process exists for this very purpose, and we rely on transparent public debate and the popular will to keep leaders in check. The voters must review the president's conduct and decide whether Donald Trump is fit for office, whether he embodies the American spirit, and whether we will allow the behavior of one man to define us as a whole.

The solemn responsibility rests with each of us. By definition, an *electorate* is the sum of the people in a nation entitled to vote. In the United

States, approximately 75 percent of the population is of "voting age," but turnout tends to be closer to 50 percent. That means in our upcoming and highly contested presidential race, half of the country will make a momentous decision for the others. One half will define us all.

We must remember that we are whom we elect. "Like man, like state," Plato wrote two millennia ago. "Governments vary as the characters of men vary. States are made out of the human natures which are in them." The government of the United States is whatever it is because the people are whatever they are. The nature of one man, the president, is not what shapes the collective attributes of a nation. It is the other way around. Our views, our aspirations, and our morality are what define the republic and are meant to be reflected by the people we elect.

On voting day, we will have had four years to make up our minds about Donald Trump. Entering the booth, there will be many factors to weigh when considering whether to reelect him to the presidency. Is he more qualified than the others? Is he offering a more compelling agenda? Has he demonstrated a record of success? As we stare at our secret ballots, the most important question of all will be: *Does he reflect us?*

A WARNING

There are several ways to answer the question. The first is "Yes, he does." Donald Trump reflects our nation, and therefore, the choice is obvious. The voter will seek to reelect him. He's the right guy for the job. The second is "No, he doesn't." If during one term in office, Trump has fallen short of our standards and doesn't faithfully reflect our values, there is a chance to course-correct. The electoral process doesn't pronounce a final sentence; it offers the chance to fix mistakes. The voter will choose someone else.

There is a third answer, though: "Yes, he does. But it's not acceptable." A voter may conclude that Donald Trump's roller-coaster presidency is a faithful representation of what is happening in our society. They may argue that the 2016 presidential election resulted in the elevation of a man who embodied our country's internal strife. His measure of wisdom, justice, courage, and temperance is a strong indicator of whether *we* are demonstrating those traits ourselves. Yet that doesn't mean we have to submit to the malaise. We can admit that, although we ended up with the president we deserved the first time, we want better.

A single election will not change who we are, but it can signal that we intend to go a new direction. It's only a first step. In the conclusion of this book, we will talk about the more urgent repairs needed under the hood of our republic. For now, any rehabilitation of "We the People" can begin with a declarative statement of change from "We the Electorate."

In an odd way, an even bigger worry for our republic is what may happen if Trump is removed from office—by impeachment or a narrow defeat in the ballot box—and he refuses to go. In the beginning of the administration, I could see a man still in awe that he was sitting in the Oval Office, struggling to play the role of president. No conversation was too distant from the 2016 election and how, in his view, it was nearly "stolen" from him. Deep down there was a nagging insecurity that maybe he didn't belong there. It was one reason why few dared to bring up Russia's indisputable interference on his behalf in the election. But he quickly grew accustomed to the trappings of power, the ability to summon servants or Diet Cokes with the push of a button, to show the majesty of the Oval Office to visitors, to bellow orders and expect them to be followed. Trump relishes the cocoon he has built. He will not exit quietly—or easily. It is why at many turns he suggests "coups" are afoot and a "civil war" is in the offing. He is already seeding the narrative for his followers—a narrative that could end tragically.

A WARNING

Our moment for this conversation is now. We will lose all hope of having a real dialogue within ourselves and with our neighbors in the immediate run-up to Election Day. Rationality will be locked away at that point, and our judgment will be clouded by emotion. It's always been this way in our system. If we consider our national character and that of our current president—in advance of voting—it will inform how we react in the heat of that moment. It may temper our factionalism during the race. Hopefully it will prevent us from making self-destructive choices on the ballot.

However, it will get harder by the day. The president is already attempting to intimidate voters based on cynicism and fear. With his trademark sarcasm, he is gingerly assigning comical call signs to his opponents to turn off independent voters. Trump also wants middle-of-the-road Americans to be afraid to go a new direction. "If you don't support me, you're going to be so goddamn poor," he bellowed at a campaign rally, suggesting economic ruin without him. It's become a refrain. "You have no choice but to vote for me," the president told another group of supporters, "because your 401(k), everything is going to be down the tubes. So whether you love me or hate me, you gotta vote for me."

We can't cave to Trump's elementary logic that there's "no choice" but to vote for him. He should be fired. And it's time to take stock of our options for his replacement.

The Devil We Don't Know

I cannot overstate the consequences of reelecting Donald Trump. I've seen the impact of his leadership on our government and country, up close and all too personal. The Trump administration is an unmitigated catastrophe, and the responsibility rests entirely at his feet, the predictable outcome of assigning organizational leadership to a man of weak morals. What is more regrettable is that his faults are amplifying our own. I believe firmly that whatever benefits we may have gained from individual Trump policies are vastly outweighed by the incalculable damage he has done to the fabric of our republic. I cannot yet say who will turn the ship, but four more years of Trump could very well sink it.

There is something else to consider about the next four years—how lucky we have been to avoid a monumental international crisis since Trump took office. We have not suffered a major attack against the United States or been forced to go to war, but it's only a matter of time before that luck runs out. Those of you tempted to vote to reelect Donald Trump, despite the scandals and despite credible evidence of wrongdoing, might want to consider what could happen when that crisis comes. Do we want to keep our nuclear arsenal, and our nation's military, under the stewardship of a man who ignores intelligence briefings, who puts his self-interest ahead of the country's needs during international engagements, who enjoys the company of foreign thugs, who our enemies think is a fool they can manipulate, who has shunned our friends, whose credibility has been shattered, and who our national security leaders no longer trust? Consider it.

Fortunately, there are already candidates in the race who are more honorable than the current president and stable enough to handle the demands of the presidency. With luck, the field will widen to include other public figures who appeal to both sides of our polarized electorate. I will not endorse a particular person. Every voter needs to make up his or her own mind. We don't know what the final ballot will look like, which will impact every man's and woman's considerations, but the essential point is that we cannot be afraid to make a change.

Even still, the choice will not be easy for my fellow Republicans. The race is likely to come down to two candidates. Republicans will face a trade-off: "Pick the devil I know, Donald Trump, whose views align more closely with mine but whose moral code is visibly compromised. Or pick the devil I don't, a Democrat, who will fight for policies I disagree with but is probably a more decent person." Last time around, ideology tipped the balance over temperament. A semi-Republican Trump was better than a hardcore-Democrat Clinton, the thinking went. This time Republican voters should reconsider their math.

I'm not saying it's desirable for our party to lose the White House. Most Republicans won't support the Democratic alternative to Trump, but if the other side does win, Republicans shouldn't be fearful of becoming the "opposition party." It's easier to fix mistakes wrought by bad policies than those wrought by bad people. Conservatives generally respected former president Obama as a family man but despised his agenda. In the end, a number of his initiatives were reversed as easily as the executive orders it took to establish them. Trump, on the other hand, has done far more damage because of his true nature. His innate flaws are the dark side of his legacy. They have cut to the core of our political institutions and civic life with long-lasting effects. We'd be better off as a party opposing the agenda of a weak president from the outside than apologizing for one from within. Besides, the last time Republicans were in the opposition, the GOP got pretty damn good at it.

Nevertheless, the counterargument to my point will be strong if the Democratic Party nominates someone deeply out of touch with mainstream America. Then everything changes. If it's one of the Democratic candidates preaching "socialism," Trump's fearmongering will still be persuasive. Republicans will argue that the other candidate, as president, would attack our free-market principles, tax us into economic recession, promote a thought-police culture of political correctness, fan the flames of identity politics, and bring government into our lives like never before. It will be a repeat of 2016. Compared to the leftward-lurching Democratic Party, Trump will seem friendlier to conservative ideals. Discussions about qualifications will give way to emotion and fear, and Trump's reelection chances will rise.

Democrats reading this book know how high the stakes are. I implore you, if you want a majority of our nation to reject Donald Trump, you must show wisdom and restraint in selecting your party's nominee. Resist the temptation to swerve away from the mainstream. Trust me. We flirted with extremes in the GOP during the last cycle, and look where it got us. If Democrats do the same, Trump will be that much closer to a second term and better equipped to convince Americans to stick with him. If, however, you nominate someone who campaigns on unity instead of ideological purity, you will have a sizable number of Republicans and independents ready to make common cause.

Trump or an unnamed Democrat are not our only options. If we had courage, the Republican Party would seriously consider replacing President Trump at the top of the ticket. I know firsthand that leading GOP officials would like to dump the president if there was a strong candidate willing to step forward. They talk about it behind closed doors. Many Republican senators and congressmen are itching for someone else, despite the fact that they pay homage in public to the current occupant of the Oval Office. Some former Republican officeholders have announced primary challenges to the president. More may throw their hats into the ring before this is published. These candidates have obvious shortcomings, but Republicans should ask themselves, are those shortcomings more numerous than those our commander in chief has displayed already? Not by a mile, which is why the alternatives to Trump should be taken seriously.

In the end, if the Republican Party refuses to stand up to the president, and if the Democratic Party cannot nominate a candidate that appeals to both sides of our divided society, then we are in dire need of a leader bold enough to break the two-party system. There is an opening for an independent candidate ready to put country before party. He or she should be a leader whose *platform* is America's *common ground*, not one of the respective tribal camps in US politics. A credible third-party candidate will find support from silent Republicans eager for an alternative, Democrats uninspired by their field, and independents desperate to break free of this mess.

Americans worried about a second term of Donald Trump have another choice on Election Day I've not yet mentioned. There is one final option for preventing him from wreaking havoc for another four years if he's reelected. It's an insurance policy, and it will be right in front of you when you step into the voting booth. Look down. Democracy's next-best safeguard is the rest of the ballot.

You will have a slate of aspiring public officials to choose from who can hold the US government accountable. Don't focus solely on your pick for the nation's highest office and play roulette with the rest of the candidates running for the US Senate, the House, state offices, and so on. You must consider which of these people are ready to lead. Are they prepared to keep the president and our executive branch in check? Will they be unafraid to speak the truth? Do they have the honorableness and decency that have become endangered traits in today's politics? If we exercise good judgment on the rest of the ballot we can better protect our country's institutions and its future.

No matter what happens on Tuesday, November 3, 2020, Americans have another pressing review to conduct. It's bigger than a presidential election. This particular duty doesn't involve weighing individual candidates, or anyone running for public office for that matter. The task at hand is to judge someone far more important than the commander in chief, someone who will be illuminated by the national spotlight whether or not Donald Trump is reelected. Ourselves. The time has come to assess the civic fault lines spreading across our republic.

A Warning

The character of one man has widened the chasms of American political division, but if any good comes from the turmoil, hopefully it will be that it causes us to reinvestigate—and reinvigorate—the character of our nation.

EPILOGUE

"We are not enemies, but friends. We must not be enemies. Though passion may have strained, it must not break our bonds of affection. The mystic chords of memory will swell when again touched, as surely they will be, by the better angels of our nature."

—*Abraham Lincoln*

Let's roll." Those were Todd Beamer's final words before he set down the phone.

Todd was an account manager for a computer company, and his early-morning business trip came on the heels of a five-day vacation in Italy. He and his wife had just returned the night before. Rather than take off immediately to his next destination, he spent the evening at home with her and their two children.

Now Todd was midair on the way from Newark to San Francisco, and his plane had just been hijacked.

About forty-five minutes into the flight, four men stormed the cockpit, slitting the throats of the pilots and taking over the aircraft. One of them made an announcement over the intercom in broken English: "Ladies and gentlemen: here the captain. Please sit down, keep remaining seating. We have a bomb on board. So sit."

They herded passengers into the rear of the jet and banked back toward the East Coast.

Todd tried to use the seat phone and was connected with Lisa Jefferson, a call center representative for the in-flight phone company. He calmly described the scene for her to relay to authorities. The men had knives out. One appeared to have a bomb strapped to his body. The pilots were lying motionless on the floor. A fellow passenger had been killed.

Todd's seatmates received word via calls to loved ones that the World Trade Center and the Pentagon had been struck by hijacked airplanes. The passengers and crew huddled to discuss the situation. They didn't want to be the next aircraft flown into a target, so they took a vote and agreed to retake the cockpit.

Todd informed Lisa, who was still on the line, that they planned to wrest control of the plane back from the hijackers. He asked her to do him a favor. If he didn't survive, he wanted her to call his wife with a message: "Tell her I love her and the boys." She promised she would, but what Todd would never know was that his wife was pregnant with a baby girl, too. He recited the Lord's Prayer and Psalm 23.

"You ready?" he asked fellow passengers. "Okay. Let's roll."

They rushed the front of the plane. A few minutes later, after a struggle in the cockpit, United Flight 93 crashed into an open field in Somerset County, Pennsylvania, about twenty minutes flying time from Washington, DC. All souls onboard perished.

The story of Flight 93 filled Americans with solemn pride in the painful days after the attacks of September 11, 2001. In the face of terror, the passengers displayed moving bravery. These everyday heroes undoubtedly saved many lives, diverting an airplane before it could become a missile, one that was reportedly bound for the US Capitol Building. Theirs was the true American spirit, and it far eclipsed the cowardice that briefly controlled the skies that fateful morning. In the aftermath, the words of Todd Beamer became a rallying cry for a more united country.

Most recall the months after 9/11 as a period of patriotic renewal in the United States. We flew flags outside our homes. We held our families closer. We felt an unspoken connection to strangers like never before—simply because they were fellow Americans. The sudden embrace of unity over division was not inevitable, as less than a year earlier the nation was split by one of the most fiercely contested elections in history. But after the attacks, we consciously put aside our differences, a collective act facilitated in part by a president's unifying rhetoric. In an address before Congress on September 20, 2011, President Bush stoked the embers of a common bond, telling Americans we would come together against the threat of violence from terrorists. "We will not tire, we will not falter, and we will not fail."

Now imagine the scenario played out differently. Pretend that instead of resolve, Bush expressed skepticism after 9/11. Imagine that, as smoke rose from the Twin Towers, he questioned whether al-Qaeda really orchestrated the attacks; he dismissed the intelligence community's conclusions as "ridiculous"; he suggested the hijackers on Todd Beamer's flight could have been from "a lot of different groups"; he fanned the flames of conspiracy theory by calling the incident a "hoax" and a "ruse"; he declared at a press conference, "Osama bin Laden says it's not al-Qaeda. I don't see why it would be," in response to increasingly irrefutable evidence of the terror group's responsibility; and he urged Americans that it would be a mistake to go after al-Qaeda because the United States had the potential for a "great relationship" with them. If that's what Bush had done, the political explosion would have torn the country to shreds.

That's effectively what happened when the United States was attacked in 2016. This time, the hijackers were hackers, and the president was Donald Trump. After Russia's deliberate and coordinated assault on US democratic elections, recall that Trump downplayed the incident and dismissed the intelligence community's conclusions; he questioned whether the interference was perpetrated by Moscow; he speculated that others could have been behind it; he promoted conspiracy theories; he said he believed Putin's word that Russia was not responsible; and he suggested it would be a mistake for the United States to ruin the possibility of a good relationship with Moscow over the matter. The collective national reaction was not the patriotism, unity, and resolve of 9/11. It was internal conflict, and in the meantime, the Russians got away with it.

The two attacks reveal a lot about our choices. In both cases our enemies wanted to spark chaos in our democracy. In both cases we had the option to let them, or not. I wish the passengers of Flight 93 could have seen the influence of their example upon the country in the first instance—how their courage on 9/11 became a metaphor for American determination. They would have been proud that we chose to come together rather than allow terrorism to rip us apart. I also suspect they would be dismayed to witness our equal capacity for divisiveness not even two decades after their noble sacrifice.

One might blame Trump for provoking widespread discontent instead of cohesion after Russia's interference. Go ahead and reread the above paragraph. It's still stunning to recall that this was the president's reaction. Ultimately, though, it was our choice whether to follow his lead. *We* decided to indulge in irrational speculation. *We* decided to engage in social-media warfare. *We* decided to alienate neighbors based on whether they agreed with Trump or not. Our response to the attack led to record levels of incivility.

The episode shows us why we need to broaden the national conversation beyond electoral politics. The 2020 election cycle is important and will no doubt weigh heavily on our future, one way or another, but if we want to remedy our political strife in the long run, it will not happen with a single

Election Day. The problem is much bigger than that, and the solution is not in Washington, DC.

Donald Trump got elected on the idea that our nation's capital was broken and needed a disruptor like him. "I will Make Our Government Honest Again—believe me. But first, I'm going to have to #DrainTheSwamp in DC," he tweeted on October 18, 2016, the first time he deployed a phrase that became a regular mantra. From Ronald Reagan to Nancy Pelosi, politicians have promised to "drain the swamp," a metaphor for fixing our nation's capital and getting corruption out of politics. The phrase is doubly misleading. First, it's a popular misconception that Washington, DC, was built on a swamp (it was not), and second, the metaphor presupposes our political problems are Washington-centric.

The complaint that Washington is "broken" is almost as old as our capital city itself. Little more than a decade after the US Constitution was ratified, the town was beset with rancorous political infighting. Observers lamented the "spectacle of a perpetual struggle" between the two parties, epitomized by the toxic election of 1800. "Neither reason nor justice can be expected from either side," wrote one observer, noting that personal resentments were rampant in America's political center.

Unlike our symbolic gun fights in politics today, the acrimony was so bad that it led to literal gun fights. Vice President Aaron Burr shot and killed Alexander Hamilton in an 1804 duel, in part due to simmering anger from the disputed election four years prior. If that wasn't enough to increase public disgust with Washington politicians, Burr was later arrested and indicted for treason after allegedly conspiring with fellow politicians, military officers, and foreign officials to create a breakaway republic in the center of North America. It's difficult to envision something as galling today as Mike Pence or Joe Biden devising a covert secession campaign to create their own country.

The only blip on the radar of discontent with Washington appears to be James Monroe's presidency, 1817 to 1825. These years are known as the "era of good feelings," in part because the two-party system was nearly abolished, and the nation's capital was led by a single-party government, the Democratic-Republicans. Americans were happy with their elected leaders, so much so that President Monroe ran for reelection effectively unopposed, something that hasn't happened since. But the "good feelings" were fleeting, as the issues of slavery and territorial expansion quickly polarized Washington before he left office.

Epilogue

Today the brokenness of the nation's capital is broadly accepted as a fact of life. People believe that elected officials spend too much time bickering and too little time governing. They lament the nastiness of political campaigns, the constant grandstanding, the revolving door between government agencies and industry, and the fact that compromise has become a relic of the past. You have heard it a million times before and said it yourself: "They can't get anything done."

Public trust in our government is stuck at all-time lows. A mere 17 percent of Americans believe they can count on Washington politicians to do what is right "just about always" or "most of the time," according to one poll. A vast majority of Americans—75 percent—disapprove of the job Congress is doing. Pollsters have cleverly demonstrated that the legislative body is less popular than root canals, cockroaches, and used-car salesmen. Hence, calls to "drain the swamp" resonate widely. The only branch of government with majority approval right now is the one led by *unelected* officials, the US Supreme Court.

Americans do not need to grasp blindly in the dark to find the boogeyman that is haunting our civic lives. We need only to look in the mirror. Our representatives are not the source of

Washington's problems. We are the ones who pick them. If you can give the Founders credit for anything, the democratic system reflects the public mood. When we are willing to compromise, our representatives are, too. When we are angry and unyielding, partisan and greedy, they will display the same traits.

As a result, we are getting the presidency we deserve and the Congress we deserve. Is it not obvious that elected leaders are mimicking our behavior? Their snarky attacks and Twitter jabs sound a lot like the text messages we send, the comments we make below news articles, and the condescending memes we post to Facebook because it's easier to fire rounds from behind a digital wall than hash out problems face-to-face. It's no wonder people think Washington is broken. *We* are broken.

Traveling America in the 1830s, Frenchman Alexis de Tocqueville observed, "In America the president exerts a very great influence on affairs of state, but he does not conduct them; the preponderant power resides in the national representation as a whole. It is therefore the mass of people that must change, and not only the president, in order that the maxims of politics vary." We can drain the swamp if we want by firing Donald Trump and electing a new Congress. I strongly believe the first action will make a difference. But lasting change will require deeper, nationwide self-reflection. It will require us to alter ourselves—to consider who we *were*, who we *are*, and who we *want to be*.

De Tocqueville noted during his visit to the United States that the people he encountered really knew what it meant to be citizens. Ask any American about their country, he wrote, and the person will teach you about their rights, duties, and the law. He marveled at how we derived our knowledge not from books but from firsthand experience. "It is from participating in legislation that the American learns to know the laws, from governing that he instructs himself in the form of government. The great work of society is accomplished daily before his eyes and so to speak in his hands." An observer would be hard-pressed to say the same about us today.

The United States is an exceptional nation, but it could soon run the risk of civic-moral bankruptcy, the consequence of losing touch with history. The majority of Americans are unable to pass basic civics exams and know far too little about our past and our form of government. Many of us can't name our congressman or state representative, let alone describe principles such as habeas corpus or popular sovereignty. We have forgotten about the world we built yesterday. Now our tomorrow is in doubt.

There are two choices. We can either bury our heads in the sand, hoping it gets better by itself. Or we can recognize the situation for what it is and, rather than allow political turmoil to hasten our demise, begin a restoration. It's time to start searching for guideposts to rejuvenate public life. We need a "civic renaissance" for our day and age. That's how we'll right the ship. It requires dusting off the lessons of our forebears—updating them for the modern world—and reinvigorating active participation in our civic life. The topic itself deserves a separate book entirely.

To start with, we need to restore a climate of truth by clearing the air of misinformation and changing how we report, consume, and share news so we aren't living in different realities. We must also re-learn the art of "agreeing to disagree" with people whose political views we don't share, rather than alienating them. If we escape our echo chambers it will make it easier to cooperate on issues large and small. It's likewise important for us to begin re-associating in person. Our proclivity to participate in voluntary organizations was long a defining aspect of the American story, and we've been called a "nation of joiners," a trait that has allowed us to develop a democratic culture unlike any other. Sadly, our growing *interconnectedness* online is making us *disconnected* from one another, so we must find new ways to engage.

Additionally, it's time to bring the focus of politics closer to home. Our problems won't be solved with one-size-fits-all DC fixes. Washington is slow and cumbersome, and we don't have to wait for it to act. We can have a faster and deeper impact on the issues we care about—health care, crime, or drug use—by acting within our communities today. At the same time, it's incumbent upon us to focus on educating the next generation about their democracy.

I will never forget one of my first US history classes. My teacher was a veteran who had fought in the war, had scars to show for it, and ran a tight ship in the classroom. One day I got in trouble for interrupting another student. "Damn it," my teacher said, silencing the classroom. "Apologize now—*now.*" I apologized to my fellow student, but the teacher told me I also owed an apology to Thomas Paine, the American revolutionary whose writings we were studying. That and much more, he said. "Uh, what else do I owe him, sir?" I added, probably to a few chuckles. He stared me straight in the eyes and said two words I will never forget: "*Your life.*"

Our job as citizens is two-fold. We need to preserve the republic for ourselves *and* get ready to pass it along. It won't be in our custody forever. There's a US senator in Washington fond of the saying: "When you're going down a dirt road and see a turtle atop a fence post, chances are that turtle didn't get there by itself." Our country has been saved, time and time again, by the generations that picked us up before we could get run over. Now it's our turn to do the same for the next generation. We need to get serious about preparing our children for the biggest job title they'll ever have—citizen. It's no exaggeration to suggest, as my teacher once did, that our very lives depend on it.

America's past is its lodestar. Every lesson we need for renewing our country is there, waiting to be rediscovered. The shared values around which it was founded are the true north that united the states and to which we must return to preserve our future. The survival of our democracy is not inevitable. Martin Luther King Jr. famously said, "The arc of the moral universe is long, but it bends toward justice." He may be right, but it doesn't bend itself. History doesn't make us. We make history. Its course is changed by the people themselves who, with their values as a sextant, navigate daily moral quandaries. The choices we make define our direction and who we are. Right now we face two momentous ones. The first: Is a man fit or unfit to be president? And the second: Are we worthy or unworthy of the blessings of liberty? One will be decided by ballot and the other by our behaviors in the weeks, months, and years to come. I hope you will debate the answers beyond these pages.

If we look within ourselves and undertake the arduous task of moral repair, America can restore the soul of its political system. We can once again illuminate a pathway for others onto the vaunted plazas of open society. If, however, we shrink from the task, our names will be recorded by history as those who didn't pass the torch but let its light expire. That is my warning. Every American generation before us faced and passed this test. Our charge is to do the same, proving that the United States can do what other civilizations could not—survive the ages—and bend the arc of the moral universe toward the value that is the real sinew of civic life: freedom.

Let's roll.